Babsie, Go Teach My People

Babsie, Go Teach My People

by Ursula Marie-Crescence Bleasdell

with Laurie Watson Manhardt

FRANCISCAN UNIVERSITY PRESS
Franciscan University of Steubenville
Steubenville, OH 43952

Published by:
  Franciscan University Press
  Franciscan University of Steubenville
  Steubenville, OH 43952
  Printed in the United States of America

Cover design: Marie Shively
Cover photos: Steve Zehler

  ~~BN 0-940535-96-3~~

Dedicated to the Immaculate Heart of Mary,
my mother, godmother, two daughters,
and the countless other women who have been a
source of encouragement and hope to me.

Thanks to Laurie Manhardt who
motivated me to complete this writing.
A special thanks to Celeste Fortenberry and
Dawn C. Harris for their expertise in editing th

CONTENTS

1

My Land, My People, My Family

I come from Trinidad, a little island in the warm waters of the Caribbean off the coast of Venezuela—so small that you might think that God couldn't find it. This is the land of the hummingbird and lush vegetation, the land of steel band and calypso.

Trinidad and Tobago were discovered by Christopher Columbus in 1498. He wasn't searching for us, but he was happy to find us anyway—beautiful islands sprinkling the Caribbean, islands kissed by the sun, spanned by virgin forests, and filled with the musical sounds of rippling waters.

When Columbus sighted what he thought were three peaks, he was reminded of the Trinity; he called our island "The Land of the Holy Trinity." There is an old tale, that in his exuberance at arriving there after a difficult journey, he said to God, "I dedicate these islands you, and I ask that you will spare them from all na disasters for a thousand years." God answered him, "No, Christopher, not a thousand years, only five hundred years. After that the people will have to make their own choice."

The original Carib natives were a fierce race. They fought for their lives against the Spaniards, even choosing death over slavery. Later the French and the English arrived; then slaves from Africa; and then indentured laborers from India. Others came from China and from Lebanon and Syria, seeking sanctuary. From every country of the world people came searching for a haven among our islands. God gradually broke down the barriers of ethnic background and culture until we forgot where we came from, and knew only what we had become—one family. In its people Trinidad has become what its name implies: the land of the Trinity. We represent in microcosm what the people of God will be like on the day when the Lord comes to collect his children.

In my own bloodstream flow the indomitable blood of the Carib, the strength and power of the African, and the romance of the Spanish and French. I am the living result of Caribbean love and friendship.

My father, Woodford Edward Barnes, was African and French. His mother was very black, and his father was half French and half African. My mother, Josephine Rodriguez, was Carib, French, and Spanish from Venezuela. I was born at home, their seventh child and second daughter, on the Feast of Corpus Christi, June 16, 1921. Since there was no scale in the house, I don't know exactly how big I was; my mother guessed that I weighed about nineteen pounds.

Aunt Mildred, my father's sister, came to see me. I was sleeping in a basket in the living room. She peeped at me, then went to congratulate my mother.

"And where is the baby?" Aunt Millie asked.

"You walked right past her in the living room. Didn't you see her?"

"There was a baby sleeping, but that baby must be about two months old. I want to see the baby that was born today." She returned to the living room, laughing as she lifted me out of my basket. "How could you be so big?"

That is a reproach I have heard all the days of my life. Through elementary school, the children would tease me because I was so big, and they refused to believe that I was the youngest in my class. "But you're not counting the years you spent in jail!" my classmates taunted. Only my birth certificate convinced them.

Even today I am teased about my size. I have concluded that God provided these big shoulders so his people could find a place to weep, and these strong arms to cuddle and comfort his little ones.

My Given Name

I was baptized Ursula Marie-Crescence on Santa Rosa Day, August 30, in Santa Rosa Church, the same church where my paternal grandparents had been married ar where my father had been baptized fifty-four ye before. Can you believe I had to go almost three months without being christened? My parents delayed my baptism until the patronal feast of the parish, when there could be a festive gathering of family and friends from everywhere. After all, it had been more than a decade since they had enjoyed the blessing of a girl child.

Irene Jane, my sixteen-year-old sister, was proud to have another girl in the family. She ran and asked Rita "Romain" Lafon, the daughter of a plantation owner, "Will you be godmother for my new baby sister?"

"Did your mother send you, child? Have you asked your mother's permission? It is your mother who must make such an arrangement."

Irene ran home to ask Mama, who agreed to Irene's choice. Romain became my beloved "Nen Ro." ("Nen" is short for "Nen nen," a title for "godmother.")

Nen Ro was a lady. Like my father, she came from a family of plantation owners. She couldn't stand my father and his five brothers—all so handsome and so arrogant. But she was friends with Aunt Millie and Irene. Every Sunday morning after Mass, all the children would go to the family house and visit with the grandparents and family friends. Irene became acquainted with Aunt Millie's fashionable friend Romain and grew to love her.

Nen Ro's two sisters had married men who frittered away her father's money and property. Determined that her father's goods not be squandered by another shiftless son-in-law, she decided never to marry unless her ·itor presented her with worth comparable to her own. ᐟo you think I'm not married because no one ever asked me?" Nen Ro often asked. "Now, if you tell me I can't get to heaven unless I'm married, then perhaps I'll reconsider."

Nen Ro always opened her home to those who needed a bed and found a place at her table for those who were hungry. Although she recognized people's foolish decisions and imprudent behavior, she was always there to lend a helping hand, especially to children. She was so generous and charitable that many people called her "Auntie." All through my life I benefited from my godmother's example and charity.

A Suitable Nickname

Although I was baptized Ursula, very soon I was nicknamed "Babsie." Papa had a friend, Johnny Marcel, who trained horses, and we lived just outside the race track. He was married, but never had any children. Since I was the first girl in the family for a long time and since I woke up smiling and rarely cried, I became everyone's little doll. Johnny often would carry me over to his digs and play with me and then carry me back. The horse owner, Johnny's employer, was a white man who lived in the city and had a beautiful little daughter named Barbara, nicknamed Babsie. Johnny decided that I reminded him of that little white child. When he would steal me away to keep him company, he would call me "Babsie." And it stuck! I have never been able to shake this nickname—I believe this must be the name

God knows me by. (I even call my guardian angel "Barbie.")

My father owned and managed a small general store that sold food and basic commodities. We lived behind the store. My mother worked as housewife, mother, and seamstress. We usually had household help to do the laundry and the heavy cleaning. My little sister, Baby (Callistra Helen, named after my father's mother), was two years younger than I. Since Baby had poor health and respiratory problems, she was always on my mother's knees or in my mother's arms. So my sister Irene became my "little mother."

Childhood was lots of fun. We lived two blocks from the railroad tracks. Every day buggies (no cars at that time) traveled between the railroad and the town. There was also a river close by, where we would picnic many Saturdays. I was always running, always playing, jumping, and climbing trees; I bore the marks of childhood, always bruised. Papa called me "Acholohan" after one of his favorite race horses, whose knees were always bandaged from falls.

First Lesson in Discernment

Early one Sunday morning when I was about three years old I found my father in the kitchen marinating meat, as he often did Sunday mornings. He was cutting ๆ something red.

said, "Papa, 'matoes?" [tomatoes]

He said, "No, baby, pepper."

I said, "'matoes, please?"

"No, pepper. Burn you."

"Please Papa, 'matoes?" I stretched out my hands and cried furiously.

Since I would not be consoled, he cut off a sliver about as large as a paring from a fingernail and dropped it into my open mouth. That tiny piece set my mouth on fire. My crying turned to screams of pain. Mama came running to my rescue. She rushed me to the tap to ease the burning.

For nine years afterwards I didn't touch a tomato.

My father taught me a quick lesson in discernment—tomatoes and peppers might look alike, but they taste entirely different. All that is red and shiny is not sweet and tasty! Since he could not convince me by his words, he needed to convince me by experience. God sometimes works the same way. If only we would hear God's word and respect it, we could avoid many a painful experience. God acts only out of love—and in his love he is so committed to our salvation that he pursues us relentlessly until we learn the vital principles of life.

My mother used to say, "Those who can't hear will feel." I have learned many things in my life through the hard school of experience. Priceless pearls of wisdom have been hidden in each experience. Each one has melted and molded me and brought me to the place where I understand that everything God does for us is done out of his great love. No matter how we experience it, God only acts out of love.

2

The Great Depression

In those days parents didn't talk much in the presence of children. Nevertheless, we children sensed a cloud lowering over our household. We noticed the store had fewer sweets for us to steal for our friends and less stock on the shelves. The depression that struck the United States had worldwide ramifications. My family and my father's shop experienced them. Soon I began to hear a word that I didn't understand: bankruptcy.

Then one day the shop was closed and we moved to quarters two blocks away—a lovely three-bedroom house that we rented for six dollars a month, right next door to the Moslem mosque. Every month the family worried over how to pay the rent. My mother sewed beautiful dresses for one shilling (twenty-four cents) each. My father went to a town in the south of the island called Siparia to work as a mercantile clerk a job at which he was well versed. Papa had a gift persuasion. Once he told me that a lady came buy pajamas to bury her husband in and Papa sold her two pairs!

Work in Siparia took Papa away from home for the whole week. My oldest brother, Sylvester, became father in his absence. He had acquired my father's heart and he knew our father's mind, and he was given full authority to govern us children, to punish, to praise, to reward, or whatever.

Cyril Joins the Police Force

My second oldest brother, Cyril, was sixteen and was a pupil-teacher at the Roman Catholic boys' school. He earned two dollars a month from the parish priest. Cyril decided, without letting my parents know, to seek entry into the Trinidad police force. The minimum age was eighteen; but he was so tall and athletic and well-educated that he felt he could present himself to the police chief for selection. While Cyril was standing in line, a sergeant (who was a friend of the family) recognized him. But the commissioner who was interviewing the boys never asked Cyril for a birth certificate.

Cyril came home with the news that he had been accepted into the police force. Absolute mourning enveloped the household. My father knelt down and wept, thanking God that his mother had not lived to see this dishonor that had been visited upon our family. It was the first time I saw my father cry. To be a policeman was the last thing for any son of a decent family to choose.

My brother remained resolute. My mother knew his schedule, and every night that he was on duty she would stay awake and pray, unable to sleep while her son was out on the streets. Then she worked all the next day as if she had slept all night.

The police commissioner took an intense interest in this young man, who was obviously beyond the run-of-the-mill. He invited Cyril to lime (what we say in Trinidad to mean "hang out") with his own sons, hockey players; and thus Cyril became one of the first local black boys to play hockey in the islands. He soon became island champion and was known for his expertise in goal-keeping. He represented the country in the Caribbean as a hockey player. He also became police department champion in running and other sports. Later my father's grief and mourning turned to joy and dancing when at twenty-one Cyril was raised to the position of drill instructor for the Trinidad police force, moving off the police beat and enjoying the respect of the officers on the police force.

The Trap of Illegitemacy

Eventually we moved to a house on thirteen acres of land within the town limits. Fruit trees everywhere beckoned me to climb them and helped me to become a veritable tomboy. At this time our family gained two new members.

My oldest brother Sylvester, twenty years old, was Saint Jude's College with the Anglican canon, Rever

Merry. Handsome Sylvester, gregarious and full of fun, was loved by Reverend Merry like a son. He sang in the Anglican choir and had a throng of Anglican girls chasing him. He became friendly with one of them, Edna.

Like a good mother, Mama called Edna and tried to get her to see that this Casanova son of hers could do nothing but bring her trouble.

"If you hope to get anything from this relationship, guard your chastity. Don't make yourself cheap for him. He is still a boy. Who do you think buys all the clothes on his back? They are mine. I have paid for them. Don't let Sylvester make a fool of you."

Edna read into this that Mama didn't like her because she was Anglican and because she was poor. Mama's son was too good for her. But Mama really did have Edna's best interests at heart. She knew how this intensely hormonal period of life could end up: young men promised love in the heat of passion and then failed to keep their promises. Fatherless children are not at all uncommon in Trinidad.

Despite Mama's warnings, Sylvester and Edna's friendship resulted in two illegitimate children. The first, Norma, was only nine months younger than my sister Baby. My father came to the rescue. He had a strong sense of blood lines. His own mother had had the reputation of accepting any child that she was told had been fathered by one of her six sons. She would search for birthmarks on the child, and if she found them she would accept the child into the family with full ˙s. Papa inherited the same characteristic. He would put up a strong fight to avoid an issue. But once it got beyond prevention, he would accept it.

"Don't try to shut the stable after the horse is out!" Papa would proclaim.

My sister Irene was godmother for this child and Norma was absorbed into the family with full privileges. Two years later, her brother, Arnim Christopher, whom we called Sonny, was immersed into our family in the same way. When Sylvester was finally mature enough to settle down and marry, he chose the daughter of his supervisor, a well-educated city girl.

I grieved for Norma. She was so displaced. Many people thought we were three sisters, although she had much lighter skin than I, and Baby was two shades darker still. When Sylvester came home with his wife and new children, Baby and I were still free to climb upon his lap, but Norma would slink into the background, embarrassed in the company of his new and favored children. The shame of illegitimacy stung me deeply. I discovered in those days that a grandfather's love could never make up for a father's absence. Right then I vowed that I would never, ever be a single parent. Never. Never. Never.

Departure of My Little Mother

When I was six my sister Irene became engaged to be married to my father's nephew, my cousin Andrew Irene's wedding provided one of my favorite childho memories with the dressing up and the baking the festivities associated with planning a large family wedding. Baby, Norma, and I would be little bridesmaids. We enjoyed trying on fancy clothes and planning the wedding and carrying my sister's train up the aisle. Everyone was sewing and happy. But on the wedding day itself, December 27,1927, I shed many tears. Irene, my little mother, was moving with her new husband, a teacher, to the city. All these changes in our household overwhelmed me. I cried and cried.

Within the first year of her marriage, Irene gave birth to twins, both of whom died in the city hospital. Quickly she became pregnant again and came to Arima for my mother's comforting presence during the last months of her pregnancy. I can remember how swollen her feet were. Everyone was anxious about the possibility of kidney trouble. Normally, childbirth occurred at home, but they took Irene to the district hospital so that a doctor could attend the delivery. I looked forward to this new baby, not really understanding all the negative manifestations.

Irene was so fearful during this pregnancy. She would light a candle every day and pray and pray. One day the candle mysteriously fell across the stand, and when she came into the room, she found it burning at both ends. Irene was deeply distressed and considered it to be a premonition of impending death. It was a few days before her expected delivery.

One morning I awoke to hear my mother coming down the street, wailing at the top of her lungs, "Mary, dear other, I'll sing a hymn to thee. Thou art the Queen of ven, thou too our Queen shall be. . . . O rule us and guide us unto eternity. . . ." Mama had her hands over her head as she sang and sang. When I beheld my mother singing so loudly and inconsolably, I knew that my beloved sister and her child were dead. Later in the evening, the bodies of Irene and her baby were brought home to be laid out for the wake. All my big, strong brothers were sobbing and weeping.

The whole town came to the funeral. My brother's godfather made a white coffin and Irene was placed in it with the baby at her side. I remember well the horse and buggy hearse, draped with a heavy black lace shawl, going up the same hill that my mother had come down singing. Weeping people followed the hearse in a procession almost a mile long. Everyone who could walk attended that funeral.

For months I grieved the loss of my little mother. Moreover, I was the bronze image of Irene; when my mother would look at me she would be reminded of Irene and would burst into tears. I felt so rejected, especially since Baby was always on Mama's knee.

This happened at Easter time. By Christmas Mama was still mourning and grieving and wanted nothing to do with Christmas preparations. For Christmas we usually baked cakes and boiled ham and enjoyed delicious sweet meats. So with the approach of Christmas I asked Papa if he would buy the ingredients so I could fix them for Christmas.

"But how will you do it child?" Papa asked.

"I will ask the neighbors to help me," I said confidentl

"Atta girl," Papa praised. "That's my girl!"

3

Does God Love Black People As Much As White People?

Both my parents were part French, so we spoke French patois, a creole French, as a second language. My mother's mother was educated in French and spoke very little English. She prayed in French; my first experience of the rosary was in French.

It was common for Papa to point out the good characteristics of each race and exhort us to emulate them. Sometimes my brothers and sisters and I would take the candy from Papa's shop to share with our playmates. When he caught us, he would scold us: "When the Indian and Chinese children live in stores, they sell their parents' goods. The Indian and Chinese children protect their parents' property. Whereas the African children give away their substance. We will always be poor unless we take a page from their book and learn from them."

For him, each human being had the dignity of b‿ created in God's image and likeness. Papa consider‿

dignity above money, race, and class. And to make us comfortable in the castle of our skin, he would often affectionately call us "nigger." People often don't understand this. But he knew that somewhere along the way someone would call us that to hurt us, and he wanted to desensitize us. So he played around with us. "Nigs" became a nickname between my father and us. Papa inoculated us against racial prejudice, bigotry, and intolerance. We didn't mind being black, being niggers, being anything. We were "Barnes!" Later he would make the littlest grandsons pat their chests and boast, "I am big Barnes!" even while we were living in genteel poverty.

But whenever he needed to correct us, he would call us by our full Christian name, and we would respond, almost with a click of the heels and a salute. We knew when he meant business. He was a great disciplinarian.

Papa had another strategy for preparing us for life. Whenever he felt that our hours of play outweighed our studies, he would admonish us, "All play and no work makes Jack a dull boy. Time to stop playing and start studying. If you just play and don't study, you will never get anywhere. All your little light-skinned cousins have their passports to get into the bank and work fine jobs, but without an education, you will only become a counter jumper!"

Education, discipline, and respect were essential for success in our lives, and Papa knew it. He was aware of racial prejudice, but he never allowed us to wallow in self-ty. He made us take responsibility for our lives. He im-ed to us the confidence that all men are created equal;

if we lived right and worked hard, we could achieve our full potential.

When I was two and half, I was eager to be in school. (Kindergarten starts early in Trinidad.) The older children walked me about a mile and a half to the Arima girls' convent school, run by the Sisters of Saint Joseph of Cluny. They all were white Irish nuns, intense in religious fervor and committed to academic excellence. They taught with a dedication and gentleness that has affected my whole life. I remember them with deep gratitude.

The nuns taught that we all were meant to get to heaven. I liked to read about the saints. I used to feel I would like to be a saint, but I didn't see any black ones. That became a stumbling block: "Well, that's not for me. I am black and there are no black saints." I strove only for the least that I could get in the kingdom of God—heaven. I assumed that I would have to be white to become a saint. No one told me this, I just inferred it.

"Does God love black people as much as white people, children?" asked the nun.

"Yes, Mother," responded all the children in my catechism class.

"If you cut a black man and a white man, will you find the same red blood running?"

"Yes, Mother."

"Can black people and white people get to heaven?"

"Yes, Mother."

Nevertheless, there was a subtle, unspoken prejudice underlying everything. At the time of the Corpus Christi feast, children dressed as angels and marched in

procession, throwing flower petals for the Blessed Sacrament to pass upon. Mother would go to all the classes
and choose suitable candidates to be angels. She always
chose the lightest-skinned children with soft curls. We
never thought this was odd because we had never seen a
picture of an angel being anything but white with soft,
blonde hair. But one lively little girl in my class, Balbina
deGraf, with ebony skin and tight, kinky hair, ran forward and grabbed Mother by the sleeve.

"Please, Mother, I want to be an angel," she begged.

"Oh, child, there are no black angels, dear," gently ad-
monished the nun.

The whole class laughed and I laughed with them. How
could Balbina have been so foolish?

I experienced the same subtle rejection when selections
were made for the Christmas pageant. We, the darker-
skinned children, comprised the choir. The lighter-
skinned ones who lacked talent joined us. But no matter
how talented we dark-skinned children were, we would
never be chosen for the dramatic parts. I longed to be in
the drama. My ability to recite was great, but I knew I
would never be chosen. My lighter-skinned cousins with
much less talent would regularly be selected. Because of
this—in spite of my father's convictions—I had an un-
true sense of my own worth as a person.

At home, too, we received Catholic formation. We
knelt together and prayed our prayers aloud so our parents could hear us—they never trusted us to say our
prayers alone. We walked to Mass together every Sun-
The parish priest quizzed me on my catechism

lessons before allowing me to receive First Holy Communion and Confirmation. Even if I didn't understand them, I knew all the answers! In my *Little Key of Heaven* prayer book, there was a prayer to become a saint. I mumbled through this because I did not want to pray impossible prayers even at this tender age of seven years.

The nuns marched us to confession the first Thursday of each month to prepare us to receive Holy Communion in a state of grace each first Friday. After confession, Mama would not allow us to go out to play, lest we sin and lose our absolution. Perhaps she thought our absolution was like marbles in our pockets ready to tumble out if we jumped or ran.

God used all these experiences to prepare me for the revelation of his plan. In the fullness of time he brings about what he wants. First he makes us thirsty: "Blessed are those who hunger and thirst for righteousness, for they shall be satisfied" (Mt 5:6 RSVCE). He was stirring up in my heart the desire to be a saint. But I tried to suppress this desire. I knew there were no black saints.

At last I saw a picture of Saint Martin de Porres—many, many years later. There it was—a black face staring up at me, and "St." in front of his name! He and the martyrs of Uganda blew the myth of the absence of black saints. God really wants me to be holy, and he has reserved for me a place in the gallery of saints if I want it.

At a prayer meeting in Canada a number of years ago, a woman read, "Blessed be the God and Father of our Lord Jesus Christ, who has blessed us in Christ with every spiritual blessing in the heavenly places, even a chose us in him before the foundation of the world, that we should be holy and blameless before him" (Eph 1:3–4 RSVCE). For the first time those words struck my heart. The nuns of my youth had assured me that Mary had been chosen by God before the foundations of the world were laid. This night a light turned on in my heart and I realized that I, too, had been chosen by God before the foundations of the world were laid. What was more, at the time he chose me, God invested me with every grace and blessing necessary for me to become holy and blameless and live in his presence. As the woman read on, I wanted to jump up, clap my hands, and shout, "Have you heard it! Have you heard it! The grace is already invested in us. All we've got to do is discover it, accept it, and use it. God wants us to be holy because he is a holy God."

Holiness is not something I work on. Holiness is something I desire. Holiness is something I acquire by gazing on God and desiring him.

4

A la Volunte de Dieu

When I was seven years old I made my first confession, received my first Communion, and was confirmed—in those days we did all three within a short period of time. I and my classmates made our first Communion at the seven o'clock Mass, were confirmed at ten o'clock the same day, and at three o'clock renewed our baptismal promises and made a vow to Mary.

We sang, "The vow is made and we belong to Mary. Our hearts are hers. To her we give our love. Life is but short to offer in her service. Even in death, our loyalty we'll prove. The vow is made. We'll break it never. Mother of God, we are thine forever." I think our Lady took that prayer seriously and remained with me in the most difficult times of my life.

I continued to go to the convent school. I learned my poems well and recited them for Papa and his friends. One of my favorite poems was called "The Bird." I can't remember the author, but it goes like this:

The Bird
I lived first in a little house
and lived there very well.
The world to me was small and round
and made of pale, blue shell.
I lived next in a little nest
nor needed any other.
The world to me was made of straw
and covered by my mother.
One day I fluttered from the nest
to see what I could find.
The world to me was made of leaves.
I have been very blind.
At last I flew beyond the tree
and saw the sky so blue.
Now how the world is really made
I cannot tell, can you?

As I recited this poem I would toss my little head and
shake my shoulders. Papa would say, "Atta Girl." This was
a happy time of my life. I had a strong sense of my father's
love and protection.

Every August we celebrated the Santa Rosa Festival.
People came from all around for the horse races, circuses,
and food. And the parish had a procession in which the
Carib people paraded with the statue of Santa Rosa, who
was allegedly of Carib origin. The festival started with
Mass in the morning, followed by a luncheon with stalls
of every kind, including food and desserts and local art,
to raise funds for the parish. We could never enjoy the

luncheon as a family because of our lack of money, but my father always went as a token presence. We children ate at home after the big procession and then returned to enjoy the music and dancing. How I longed to feast at the parish lunch! I observed the town doctor and his wife and two children sitting together at the table; in my childish mind it seemed that the only way I would ever be able to attend the parish luncheon with my family would be if I married a doctor. This became my dream. Every time we played doll's house, I became the doctor's wife; I walked proudly and carried my dolls around in a little carriage fashioned out of a shoe box.

Enjoying Genteel Poverty

We had no television, no radio, no electricity at that time. The better families owned gas lamps and everyone else used kerosene lamps. At different times our family had both. We created our own entertainment. At night Papa and Mama would be the audience for our impromptu plays and singing and dancing. Sunday afternoons Papa would play cricket with us. We shared meals together, making them really sacramental. Money was short, but there was always food.

There was room for everybody who came to our home. It was a common thing for my father to hand back his dinner plate to my mother so she could redistribute the food for a stranger or relative who had stopped in to visit.

Mama tried to teach us how to be thrifty, how to do

much with the little we had. We began to save a penny a day with a group of neighbors. I would go running to deposit our daily penny with the woman in charge of the "sou sou" (what we called our poor man's community bank). Every day a different member would draw the full amount to do something special.

Mama's ambition was that one of us would be a teacher, another a pharmacist, and another a musician. An old man, Mr. Filogene, came every day to teach Baby and me music. I learned the violin, which he brought with him, and Baby studied the mandolin. In exchange for music lessons he received one dollar a month and his dinner every night with our family. He always wore a jacket, collar, tie, and hat. His aroma still lingers in my nostrils; he smelled musty, like old clothes—he probably had worn nothing new in years. But he had dignity. We never became proficient, but we gained an appreciation for music.

Even though none of us fulfilled her dreams, Mama was satisfied with the way God dealt with her and with us. I can still hear her say *a la volunte de Dieu* (God's will be done), her watchword in every situation.

We enjoyed a genteel poverty. "Poverty is no excuse for uncleanliness or lack of dignity," Mama insisted. I never considered myself poor; the children at school thought I was rich, because I always had hair ribbons and shoes and socks, even though sometimes the shoes had no soles but cardboard inserts. Papa's work in the mercantile trade provided Mama with the best dry goods to make dresses for us. We may have had only three dresses a year, but they were made of the best fabric available. Papa tried to develop in us a taste for fine things.

Once Papa allowed me to go to the city to buy Easter shoes for my sister and me. Proudly I exhibited my purchases.

"Babsie, you can't wear these shoes!" Sylvester exclaimed. "They're canvas, not patent leather! What were you thinking?"

I was appalled. I was crazy, passionately in love with the shoes. They were black and beige with a little heel.

"Wait until Papa sees them!" warned Sylvester.

Papa's verdict was swift. "Sylvest, you will take them back tomorrow and bring a pair of Clark's."

Sylvester bought plain, black, Clark's leather, flat-heeled shoes. No amount of pleading could persuade Papa to change his mind. Papa's house was his kingdom.

How we look and carry ourselves on the outside tells a big story about what we are like on the inside. Do not let the devil deceive you into believing that how you look has nothing to do with who you are. Men and spirits interpret by what they see. The devil cannot read your heart, but he can interpret the signs that he sees externally.

Papa's Bouts of Anger

In all these good times, we did not escape our share of family quarrels. Several times a year, especially aroun festivals, Papa would go out with Mama's broth and drink up a storm. He would come home less than sober. Normally at the end of the day we children would watch for Papa eagerly. His homecoming was our great adventure. But when we saw Papa walking so straight that he seemed to be bending backwards, we knew what was coming.

Loud and accusatory, he would be pleased by nothing. The dinner was cold and everything was wrong. He talked and talked; we became quiet. My mother kept still until he said something that so stung her that she would cut in—and all hell would break loose. Sometimes furniture flew. He was like a hurricane. I have watched him pick up the four ends of the table cloth and shake the china, glasses, food, and everything out the window like it was just crumbs.

I dreaded those times. They seemed to affect me more deeply than they did anyone else in the family. Everyone else seemed to take them in stride, but I could not. One Sunday morning after such a Saturday night, I determined that I was never going back to Mass. I was tired of praying, since nothing ever happened to change for the better. So, instead of getting dressed for Mass, I picked up a broom and started working out in the yard feverishly, transferring my anger to the broom.

"Aren't you going to Mass this morning?" Mama asked.

"I'm never going to Mass again. Never! I'm tired of praying that you and Papa will stop quarrelling—nothing happens." I resumed my angry sweeping.

Mama looked at me sadly but said nothing and returned to the kitchen to continue preparing breakfast.

She never said anything about it. But on the following Sunday I was dressing for Mass again. The sadness in her eyes and her silence had been more persuasive than any argument. She knew it. Mama was a wise woman.

Another time, distressed by my father's drinking bouts, I asked my mother, "Why did you ever live with this man?"

"For your sake, child. I always figured if it was this hard to live with the father of your children, how much harder would it be to live with a stranger? When I was twenty-three years old and I had three children, I went to the church, knelt down before the altar, and promised God that I would live my life entirely for him and for the sake of the children. I consecrated myself to Mary and sought her intercession on my behalf." That explained why she wore blue or white for several years. Later on, in the renewal of her consecration to our Lady of Mount Carmel, Mama changed and wore only brown. We never went to bed so late that Mama wasn't on her knees praying, and we never awoke so early that we didn't see Mama on her knees praying.

5

The Curse

On the way home from school one day, one of the Hindu schoolgirls, Polly, told me a tale as we passed by the house of Mrs. Prout, a Catholic lady who was the adoptive mother of one of my classmates, Eileen.

"You know, Babsie, Mrs. Prout turns into a sou-couyant* at night and steals into people's houses and sucks their blood. In fact, last Saturday night she stopped my brothers on their way home from the cinema."

"Could this be true?" I asked Polly. My eyes widened.

*A soucouyant is a bloodsucker, or vampire. It would come in the night and suck people's blood—it could suck all a person's blood and kill him. When people would wake with bruises on their bodies they would say the soucouyant had come. Some people would eat salt—the salty blood made the soucouyant vomit it. Then they would find blood on the floor or on themselves.

It would be easy to dismiss these as superstitious mumbo-jumbo but some voodoo and occult are very real—and their power do not come from above. It's interesting that people who work in and the occult do not use salt at all. And interesting that the C has rites for blessing salt—one of which can be used in Sunda

"My brothers told me so. They came home very frightened."

The following day I drew Eileen aside.

"Is your real mother still alive, Eileen?"

"Yes."

"Where does she live?"

"Up in the country on one of the plantations."

"Eileen, you must contact her and tell her you want to come back home because Mrs. Prout is a soucouyant and you can't go on living there with her." My little heart was racing with concern. It never occurred to me that she would report to Mrs. Prout what I had said.

The following Saturday morning, I was still in bed when there was a caller at the door. My father invited the visitor onto the veranda. Horror of horrors, I overheard Mrs. Prout recounting the story of the news I had broken to her adopted child.

"But this child had to have heard this from somebody," my father responded. "She is incapable of making up a story like that by herself."

I felt as if I was sweating blood when my father came to get me. He brought me out, still in my nightgown, to Mrs. Prout, and asked me to explain what had happened.

"Polly told me that Mrs. Prout turns into a soucouyant at night and sucks people's blood. And on Saturday night she barred Polly's brothers' way as they returned from cinema."

Mrs. Prout, a thin little lady, was smoking and pant-like a fire engine. She would not be appeased, in spite father's apologies. Then my father spoke to me.

"I believe you are telling me the truth, but I must discipline you. You must learn not to repeat the things that you hear other people say to you."

Papa held me by one hand and went for the family's rod of correction, a leather strap on top of the cupboard, which he had nicknamed "Pedro Moreno." He only used this in grave family crises. Papa applied Pedro Moreno to my behind. I was so humiliated, though I knew that Papa was hurt more than I was. For months afterward I would just break down and weep. When people would ask why I was crying, I would reply, "Papa beat me."

But this was not the end of the matter. Mrs. Prout went to Polly's house, which was just on the other side of the mosque, and repeated the incident to Polly's parents. When confronted, Polly lied and denied any knowledge of the whole matter. Mrs. Prout returned to our house and now accused me of being not only a talebearer, but a liar as well.

My father's deepest hatred was liars: "I hate liars! You have no cover from them. You can protect yourself from a thief, but you have no defense from liars."

Mama intervened on my behalf, shouting at Mrs. Prout, "Get out! Get out of my house! We have already punished the child. What do you expect us to do, kill her? Get out, or I'll throw you out!"

Mrs. Prout scurried down the steps to the street, then turned and screeched at the top of her voice: "She will make you ashamed of her. I will live to see men drag her in the streets like a common prostitute. She will come no good. The devil will drag her around by her tail

I didn't understand the words, but I knew they were terrible. As young as I was, I recognized this tirade as a curse. My culture is familiar with the power of curses—we have learned of it through the Bible, through the Irish who educated us, and through voodoo and shango (prohibited in Trinidad at that time, but there were still remnants). "Death and life are in the power of the tongue," says Proverbs (18:21 NAB).

Faith comes by hearing—good faith and bad faith, faith in God and faith in the evil one. So too with curses. Some come through a person who has no intent to curse—a friend, a relative; but their words may tap into some insecurity and become a self-fulfilling prophecy. "The words of a whisperer are like delicious morsels; they go down into the inner parts of the body" (Prv 26:22 RSVCE). Other curses really call upon the powers of evil.

As Mrs. Prout screamed those horrible words, I shook with fear. My mother came into my room and tried to comfort me, but could not. For the first time in my life I knew shame, confusion, and remorse. How could I ever be free from this? What humiliation had I brought upon the family? How deeply had I hurt my father, that he could spank me? For the first time I recognized the power of lies. I hadn't lied. I was the object of slander.

I had to pass Mrs. Prout's house every day on my way to and from school. In church I had to pass her pew to get to ours. In those days we paid two dollars each year r the family pew in church. My father's pew was num- two and the Prouts' pew was number four on the op- side of the aisle.

After a few weeks, when my mother realized that I was still in deep agony, she took me to the priest and asked him to pray for me. He invested me in the blue scapular of the Immaculate Conception. From then on, whenever I was within range of this woman, I would grab the scapular and say, "O Mary, conceived without sin, pray for us who have recourse to thee," repeating it rapidly until I was out of danger. My mother also taught me to pray to Saint Michael the Archangel. This was the prayer we prayed every day after Mass anyhow, but I began to invoke Saint Michael more frequently. Mama also instructed me to pray the rosary incessantly, and she taught me to pray the penitential psalms. I was plunged into continuous, intense prayer because of this trauma.

That particular experience of defenselessness against lies was repeated over and over throughout my childhood and into my adult life. This lady's curse seemed to have settled on me; I encountered similar situations so many times in my life. Perhaps I would never be free, I thought. This drove me to pray all the more.

6

More Humiliations

My time at the convent elementary school ended abruptly. My class teacher, a brilliant laywoman of whom I was very fond, enhanced my knowledge of English, math, and geography in preparation for secondary school. In a conversation with my schoolmates I recounted some derogatory gossip about one of her family members. One of my classmates told the teacher. The teacher punished me by sending me out of class, but I was so mad, I went right on home. Mama took me back to school to hear why I had been punished. When the story came out, she insisted that the teacher spank me in front of the whole school assembly, which the principal did. I was so ashamed, I refused to return to that school. My parents had to send me to the public school. A Catholic child going to public school was anathema in those days! My parents were humiliated—my mother had to receive the sacraments from a priest at a neighboring parish. Once again I had brought shame upon m family. My sin had a long tail; my family had to bear the consequences of my actions.

My Tendency to Rage

When I was about fourteen, my brother Henry, seventeen, was being privately tutored. Henry had been hit by a truck as a small child and had suffered some brain damage as a result, making his school progress slow.

One day, Henry was doing homework on the sewing machine table as I was getting dressed for school. I needed to use the sewing machine to mend my school uniform; and I was pressed for time.

"Henry, could you please move your books so that I can mend my uniform?"

Henry acted as if he hadn't heard me.

"Henry, I need to use the machine! Please move your things!"

Again there was no response. I flew into a rage. I threw his books off the machine. As he tried to stop me, I began to flay him with both hands, tearing his shirt and screaming at him. My mother came in and shouted, "Babsie, stop it! Stop it! How could you strike your big brother like that?"

I heard her, but I could not stop swinging at Henry. I felt mechanized. Mama left the room and returned from the kitchen with a machete.

"You want to kill him. This will do it much more effectively. Here." She proffered the machete. Her action shocked me into the realization that I was quite capable of murder. I broke down and wept bitterly.

Later on she talked to me about my temper, drawing to my attention that, as a woman, I could not afford to behave like my father and let my temper get the better of me. I decided that I would never lose my temper again. But this tendency to rage would surface throughout my life.

"First Love"

In kindergarten one of my friends had been a boy named Vin, the son of one of my mother's friends. The next year Vin "disappeared"—I was too young to realize that he had gone off to the Catholic boys' school while I was left in the school with only girls.

While visiting a school friend a dozen years later I met Vin again. We were sixteen now; this meeting was like Carnival, Christmas—lights went on! We were both too shy for our friendship to be overt. I demurely flirted with him, sauntering down the street in my new straight skirt, conscious of Vin noticing me. He wrote me a sweet, innocuous letter professing his love for me. My father intercepted the letter and came to me.

"Babsie, did you give this boy permission to write you?"

"No, Papa." It wasn't technically a lie, but in my heart I knew I had given him nonverbal encouragement. I recalled catching his eye as we passed on the street. I had played the coquette.

"Then I must go to see his father," announced Papa.

When he returned home, Papa said, "Well, Babsie, this young man says that you gave him permission to write you. So if you want to marry, then you don't go back to school. You stay home and learn to cook and sew and care for babies. That's what married women do and that's what you will learn to do."

Papa's mind was made up. No pleading from Mama, Sylvester, or anyone else could reverse Papa's decision. I was removed from school immediately. I stayed home for one whole term. I longed to keep up with the rest of my class and begged my classmates to share with me what they were studying. At the end of the term, Papa relented and allowed me to go back to school. By then, I had learned my lesson: You don't flirt. You don't stir up love before its proper time. There is a time for everything and a season for every activity under heaven. You stay in school and learn and enjoy it while you are young.

Racial Conflict

In 1940, when I was nineteen, I had passed my exams and was working. World War II erupted and immigrants arrived. The nearby military bases teemed with British and American servicemen. White Americans and black Americans were fighting, disrupting our peaceful lives.

One night as we were sitting with my father at the dinner table, we heard a commotion outside: a rabble with sticks were shouting. A man broke into our house and threw himself at Papa's feet.

"Stand up, man. You're a man. Get up. You kneel to no man," Papa commanded.

"Throw him out to us, Mr. Barnes," shouted the mob.

Papa stood in the doorway. "This man has sought refuge in my house and not one of you will touch him."

"But that man tried to accost a woman down the road!"

"There is a place to make your complaint and we will go there. But not one of you will touch this man until we get there." Papa put on his hat and escorted the man through the mob to the magistrate. Papa's courage and gallantry deeply impressed me. I will never forget it.

My Pledge to the Lord

In 1940 I found an old notebook and wrote (in "mirror writing") "My Pledge." I wrote that I had gone to the church and knelt before the main altar and promised God that if I didn't marry a certain person then I would never marry, that I would consecrate my life to God. I think he must have been glad for that pledge. I really feel that God hoped that I would have kept that promise.

This man was twenty-three; I was nineteen. He had very bad sight, an eye condition that no one had been able to deal with. He used to have to hold his book two inches from his eyes to read, or have people read to him. He wrote all his high school exams by having someone read the questions to him. But he was brilliant. His English and knowledge of literature were superb.

My last year at high school he taught me literature. I grew very fond of him, and he of me—sufficiently fond that we thought we would marry. Finally he said, "Babsie, I'll go to the doctor one more time. If he says to me that he can do something for my eyes, I will pursue this relationship. If not, that's the end of it because I would hate to go blind after I am married to you and you have to be responsible for my life. You deserve better than that. I feel that if I ever brought you to that I would kill myself. I wouldn't be able to live with it."

So he made his appointment to see the doctor. In the meantime Sylvester got on my case. "Listen, this man that I see you looking at is a blind man, right? I have a right to tell you that you better be careful what you are doing." I opened my mouth to tell him what was happening, but he said, "No, no. No good telling me it's your business. I know what you want to tell me: it's your business. But any business of yours is my business, and I have a right to look after my own business from now on." I shut my mouth.

The doctor's report came back. The only prognosis they could see is that he would be completely blind sometime. We parted in deep sorrow. But in the meantime I had made this pledge.

Several years later I met him in the city. He was walking up the street. I walked close to him. He was so blind he did not see me. But he still had the ability to walk alone. He looked much older. I called out, "Eastlyn!" "Babsie, how are you?" I gave him a kiss on his cheek, we both laughed, and he went on his way and I went on my way. In spite of the tragedies of my life I was so glad I had not married him!

We make the terms for God, and God in the meantime is working so hard to guide our steps and bring us into a commitment with him. If only we would let him have his own way our lives would be so much easier.

7

Courtship and Marriage

Our friend Cyril, the son of our family doctor, regularly socialized with our family. Cyril's father longed for his son to follow in his footsteps and go to medical school, but Cyril was more interested in wrestling than studying. He eventually became a champion wrestler.

One day in August 1939, Cyril rode his bicycle to our house with a friend of his, Lionel McHenry.*

"What do you think of Cyril's friend?" Baby asked after they left.

"I can't stand him," I said. "I think he's the most arrogant boy I've ever met."

Nevertheless, Lio soon was coming by to visit without Cyril. Once Lio joined our family for a holiday on the islands. Papa was swimming vigorously from one island to another while Lio was directing my attempts at diving. We were both high achievers, but Lio would settl for nothing less than perfection.

*Name has been changed.

"Good dive, Babsie, but you left a ripple. Dive again and leave no ripple."

I dove again, leaving a slight swish of water. Again it was not perfect. He insisted that I try again, instructing me to spring higher and dive deeper. I dove so deeply that I struck my head on a massive concrete piling. I thought I had shattered my skull. It seemed an age before I surfaced, bits of cement embedded in my scalp. Splitting headaches and shooting pains in my neck kept me home for weeks. The incident should have forewarned me that pleasing this man would take herculean effort. But at the time it seemed a small price for his love.

While Lio and I were riding the streetcar one day, a fly lighted on my shoulder. Lio brushed it away aggressively, saying, "I love you so much that I do not even want a fly to touch you." For a nineteen-year-old girl, this was charming, flattering. I smiled.

At a birthday party at Cyril's house, I was sitting on a rocking chair, meeting a number of city folks for the first time. Lio came and perched on the arm of the chair. I basked in the light of his presence.

"What do you really want out of life?" he asked.

"Me? I just want to be a good woman who would leave the world better than she met it and the sound of whose footsteps would kindle new hope in the hearts of those who heard them." At that moment I envisioned my mother, whose firm footsteps always alerted us to her coming.

"That's all?" he asked, obviously disappointed. "I thought you wanted a university career."

"Yes," I said, "But that's all within the context of becoming a worthwhile woman." The words of Henry Wadsworth Longfellow came to my mind:

Lives of great men all remind us
  We can make our lives sublime,
And, departing, leave behind us
  Footprints on the sands of time.

(from "A Psalm of Life")

As a worthwhile woman, whether I became world-famous or known only to my children, I knew I could fulfill those words.

Everyone in the family found Lionel charming, with the exception of Papa—he didn't like him one bit. Possibly no one was good enough for his daughter.

Lionel won the Island Science Scholarship, enabling him to attend medical school abroad. Because of the war, England was a dangerous choice for schooling. Our experience of the racial tensions between the American servicemen made the United States a dubious choice. Canada seemed safe and secure

When Lio left for McGill University in Montreal, we began a weekly correspondence.

"Babsie, you've always wanted to attend university," wrote Lionel after two years of this. "Why don't you come to Canada and we can be married and attend university together? I will write to your father and ask him."

My brother Sylvester convinced Papa to allow me to go. Then we tackled the obstacle of religion—Lionel w Anglican. But he had been taught in Roman Catk boys' schools; the brothers and priests wrote to the effect that he knew enough about Catholicism that they were confident I would be able to practice fully my Catholic faith.

And so, in August 1944, at the age of twenty-three, I left my secure home for romance, education, and adventure.

As I kissed my father good bye, he said, tears streaming down his face, "Okay, Babs, this is not what I would have chosen for you, but since this is what you want to do . . ."

Sylvester cut in. "Oh, Papa, not now. Just bless her and let her go."

And so my father blessed me, reluctantly, and I left for Montreal. It took three days to get there—I spent one night in Puerto Rico, another in Miami. This country girl had never eaten in a restaurant, never flown on an airplane, and had never stayed outside her mother's house in a hotel or anything. Academically I was bright, but in life experiences I was totally naïve. Finally I arrived in Montreal. Lionel met me at the airport in a taxicab.

In the week preceding my marriage I would stay with Aunt Helen, an elderly lady from Trinidad who had written to my parents and invited me to stay with her. She understood my parents' desire to protect my reputation and the reputation of the family.

On the way home, Lionel discussed the plans he had for us. During our conversation he questioned me.

"How much money do you have with you?"

replied, "Three hundred and fifty dollars."

"Is that all?" he asked in horror.

"What do you mean? How much I have? Or how much I've brought?"

"How much have you brought all together?"

"I have $350 in cash in my handbag, a check for my school fees, and another draft for $600 to start an account."

He breathed a sigh of relief. "Whew! If all you had was $350, I was going to suggest that we both go and commit suicide."

Somehow that joke didn't seem funny to me. A great fear sprung up in my heart. I hadn't seen this young man for two years. Had living in a big country destroyed the simplicity and finesse of a young Trinidad gentleman? Would our relationship be based on money? Perhaps I was making a big mistake. But I had (with difficulty) persuaded my parents to allow me to do this. Twice in my life I had embarrassed my family. Could I risk another humiliation by running away? I made my resolve. There would be no turning back.

When I spoke with the priest about our marriage, he informed me that we could not be married during the Mass for the Feast of the Assumption, as we had planned, since Lionel was not Catholic. He moved the wedding to the preceding day, August 14. Lionel's intense pride was deeply wounded at this. He tried to overcome his pain over what he considered to be rejection by the Church, but was unsuccessful.

Lionel and I were married in a small ceremony with only about six people attending. I became Mrs. Lionel McHenry.

8

The First Discordant Notes

The honeymoon would be short-lived. Problems immediately arose over the issue of birth control. As a non-Catholic medical student he had no qualms at all about using contraceptives. He considered it irresponsible not to take the necessary precautions.

"Lio, you know we can't use condoms."

"But you can't afford to get pregnant just now as you're beginning classes."

"But Lio, you know I am a Catholic."

And so the fighting began. Perhaps the brothers had not stressed with the boys the teachings of the Catholic Church on family planning the same way the nuns had with the girls. Or perhaps Lionel had simply discounted the teaching. As an Anglican he didn't need to concern himself.

Conflict and discord entered our marriage. All I wanted to do was to run away. When I went to confession in October, I confessed to the priest that all I thought about was divorce. I hadn't been married even three months and all I could think of was getting out. Divorce became background music in my life. But the horror of the mortification that I would cause my family kept me hanging on, hoping against hope that things would improve.

I started to gain weight rapidly. Then a skin problem developed. The doctor diagnosed me with hypothyroidism—and told me I was pregnant!

I was studying psychology and Lio was a third-year medical student. Money was tight. "Get an abortion," Lionel ordered. Although abortions were illegal at that time, Lionel knew doctors on the faculty who would be sympathetic to our plight. I refused. We argued about it for a full six months.

When I was too nauseous to fry meatballs, as was our custom on Saturday nights, Lionel refused to eat. I determined to submit to his wishes, no matter how sick I might become. We had a beautiful, new little apartment with one window in the kitchen. I fried the meat and ran to the window to gasp some fresh air in an effort to postpone the inevitable vomiting.

Each night Lionel commanded, "Mrs. McHenry, go out for your walk."

"I'm too tired."

"Mrs. McHenry, get up and go walking."

"But I've already walked a great deal today. I walked to my classes and then to the grocery store and then home."

"I insist that you go for your walk."

"Lio, I'm too tired to walk tonight. I'd like to just finish reading this book."

"Get up and get out!" he ordered and overturned my chair, thrusting me to the ground in a rage. I found myself sprawled out on the floor, frustrated and bewildered. Many, many years later a physician confided to me that at that time it was believed that excessive walking could induce a miscarriage.

I never spoke about what I was going through with Lio. I never wrote home about it. I never spoke of it to my Canadian neighbors lest that give the impression that all black men were like that—Lio and I were the first black people some of them had met. I knew my brothers were not like Lio. So I kept my own counsel.

After the sixth month he came to terms with the pregnancy and stopped trying to persuade me to get an abortion. This acceptance was symbolized in his invitation to go out to dinner.

"Let's go to Chinatown. We can have dinner there," he suggested.

I was wild with joy.

"Do you have any money?" he asked. And I gave him all the money I had. We walked down the street like young lovers, stopping to admire shop window displays in the shops. In the shops Lio began to select little blue things for our baby boy, including a little blue potty; and I nodded assent. He paid all the bills like a proud daddy.

In Chinatown we selected a restaurant. "What do you want to eat?" he asked.

"Shrimp fried rice."

"I want lobster. But I don't think we can afford it."

"What happened to all the money?"

"Well, we bought all the baby's things," Lio explained.

"But didn't you have any money of your own?"

"Yes, but it wasn't enough to do all that."

"Okay, then, let's see what we can have together. Here's a dinner for two," I suggested.

"No, I want lobster."

"Look, here's another dinner for two," I pleaded.

"But I want lobster."

I suggested every affordable combination; I held my breath as he called the waiter.

"One lobster dinner and one bowl of plain fried rice," Lio ordered.

While he feasted, the tears fell silently down my face. He didn't notice. We didn't speak. What had begun as a hope-filled adventure ended in gloom. I dragged myself home, wondering if life would ever change for us.

The next three months we squabbled over what to name our little boy. Lio insisted on "Lionel McHenry," after himself. I desperately wanted a saint's name. I would gladly have settled for "Lionel *Anthony* McHenry" if he would just include Anthony because of my childhood devotion to that saint. He wouldn't budge.

In spite of our squabbles, I still held in my heart the hope that this baby might be able to heal our troubled marriage. Perhaps our son could erase the wounds Lionel and I had inflicted on one another during the first months of our marriage. Through the nine months of the pregnancy I prayed that my hopes and dreams would be realized in the birth of our son.

9

Hope for a New Beginning

On the morning of my due date (September 15, 1945), I awoke in pain.

"Do you know what to expect?" Lionel asked.

"No."

"Well, I don't know what to expect either, so we'd better get to a doctor."

At six o'clock that evening my labor pains terminated in a tiny cry. Then—

"It's a girl!" the doctor announced.

"A girl? Unbelievable!"

"Surely you will take what you get?" asked the doctor.

"I guess so," I sighed.

Lionel was not at the hospital. Though the doctor assured me that little girls are usually their father's pride and joy, I dreaded the moment when Lionel would find out that our son was a daughter.

When he arrived he said, "Mrs. McHenry, once again

you have done what is not expected of you. What are you going to call her?"

"Erica Ursula!" I blurted—Erica in honor of a Jewish friend who had anticipated the birth of this baby almost as eagerly as I had. She had been a great source of oil on the troubled waters of my life.

"That's what I have been thinking!" His answer shocked me. In an instant the name problem was solved.

I had not written to Mama and Papa about my pregnancy because I did not want them to worry about me. Because my sister Irene had died after childbirth of a retained placenta, I was afraid my pregnancy would awaken in them the old pain and hurt. I wanted to spare them the fear and concern they would experience so far away. In fact, I had also suffered from a retained placenta, but the physicians were able to remove it. Now that the baby and I were out of danger, we cabled the good news to both of our families and sent them Erica's hospital identification tags.

Little Erica was so beautiful, so perfect in form and feature, that I marveled at the mystery of life and birth. In an instant I forgot the troubles of the past months and fell in love with Lio all over again.

Lionel, too, was consumed with joy over our new baby. The anger and agony of the past nine months vanished in the ecstasy of beholding the flesh of his flesh and the fruit of our love. I think we forgave each other everything. Hope, great hope, and the joy that comes with it filled my heart. We were on our way to a brand new life.

We had fun laughing that Erica's clothes were all blue and white and we couldn't afford to change her wardrobe. This brought about a new closeness. It seemed that our old grudges had been released. We prepared for Erica's baptism with joy. The six weeks postpartum became a new courtship.

A multicultural, multiracial group surrounded our little family with love. Erica, our Jewish girlfriend, was so thrilled to have this baby named after her that she went out and bought a brand new buggy for her. My Jamaican girlfriends hand sewed and embroidered a beautiful christening gown that has served in my family for years, even down to my grandchildren. My French Canadian girlfriend became her godmother, and the whole French Canadian family was a strong Catholic support to us.

Six weeks after Erica's birth, the very first time we came together again intimately, I became pregnant again. I concealed my pregnancy from Lio as best I could. When it was inevitable that I reveal my condition, I was surprised at his response.

"Two, a dozen, what difference does it make? Mrs. McHenry, they are cheaper by the dozen."

But tensions began to creep into our household again. We were both so young and overwhelmed by the circumstances in our lives that we barely forgave one fault before another would arise in its place. Sometimes even our attempts to spare one another difficult situations resulted in conflict.

"You know, when I took Erica for her baby shots, it

broke my heart," I mentioned to him one day. "I just hate it."

"I didn't know you felt that way," he responded. "I can take her to the doctor for you."

"Would you really? Here is the last two dollars I have."

"I have bus tickets, I don't need it," he said as he bundled up the baby.

"Well, take it just in case."

When he arrived home, he rang the bell. I opened the door and saw Lio coming up the steps, the baby in one arm and a parcel in the other.

"What's in the parcel?" I asked.

"Maple sugar! The first maple sugar is out and I bought two pounds."

"How much was it?"

"A dollar a pound."

"And you bought two pounds! You spent *all* the money? I don't even have money for the baby's milk in the morning!" I slammed the door in a rage.

Our neighbor, hearing the door slam, ran out to catch me in the hall. "Mrs. McHenry, I've been looking for you for two weeks to return the quarter I borrowed from you." The neighbor handed me a quarter, and I was reminded of God's providence in caring for us.

Once Lio sent long-stemmed red roses to my office to cheer me after one of our frequent domestic quarrels. Everyone in the office commented on what a wonderful, thoughtful husband I had. I just smiled. I knew we couldn't afford the luxury of flowers. I never thanked him. I didn't need roses. I only wanted some common courtesy and consideration.

When I failed to acknowledge the roses, Lio made an oil painting of roses and hung it in the house as if to announce that he was above reproach.

Little Erica must have sensed the tension in the household and the discord in our family. Even as an infant she would strive to be a peacemaker. She would wake up early in the morning, as babies tend to do, peep to see if we were still asleep, and then put her tiny head back on the pillow. Every few minutes she would lift her head to check on us. When she knew we were awake, she would sing out "Da, da, da!" It was a delightful game. But it was not enough to break the tension.

"Lionel is not a bad person," one of his Trinidad school professors commented. "Its just that he has such great pride, that when his pride is wounded, he goes berserk." And so it was. I now feel in the depth of my being that Lio needed deliverance. The right kind of prayers could have saved him. I understand that now. But back then I only wanted out.

Home to Trinidad

By summer 1946, I was so fearful, confused, and ashamed that I wrote to Sylvester, "I'm in trouble, bad trouble. I want to come home." The next day Sylvester wired the money for me to return to Arima. He had contacted a steamship company and was assured that there would be safe, comfortable accommodations for me and little Erica. I left Canada in pain, disappointed over the way life had gone, filled with hopelessness. I returned to the haven of my parents' home.

Three weeks later, on August 22, 1946, I gave birth to my second daughter, Greta Paula Denise, a month earlier than expected.

I will never forget how glad Erica was to see me when I returned home from the hospital. But when she beheld this tiny stranger sucking at my breast, she bent over on her little knees and wept. Here she was in a land of complete strangers, without her Daddy, and now having to share her Mummy. When I realized how this little child must be affected by our life of conflict and confusion, I wept with her. We cried and cried for our dashed hopes and dreams. Later I would know that God had counted each and every tear we shed.

At Christmas a year later, when Paula was about sixteen months old, Lio turned up unexpectedly in Trinidad. Lio was excited to see his new daughter, and greeted Paula with pleasure. He didn't seem to mind anything. Hope for a lasting reconciliation sprung anew in my heart. The holidays were a real feast for everyone—it was the first time for our families to see Lio and me and our daughters together as a family.

After two weeks Lio returned to McGill to do postgraduate work in tropical medicine. (He was a real scholar, that man.) I looked forward to his coming back after he finished his studies. I wanted to start our life all over again.

10

Confusion and Shame

In September of 1948 Lio returned to Trinidad with an appointment to San Fernando Hospital (the second largest hospital in the second largest town on the island). Back then it took about an hour and a half to travel to Arima from San Fernando. The girls and I moved to San Fernando with him. We resumed our marriage afresh.

Now my childhood dream was fulfilled. I was the doctor's wife with two beautiful children. Unfortunately my dream of luncheons together as a family at the Santa Rosa Harvest Festival would never become a reality. Church suppers were the farthest thing from Lio's expectations.

We tried to settle down to life in San Fernando, but it was difficult. We were total strangers in a new environment.

Lionel had an insatiable need to control everyone and everything in his environment at all times. He had to approve everything I wore and every purchase I made

Although I sewed beautifully, he insisted on checking the fabric and pattern before I could make anything.

One day Erica came into my bedroom and found me sewing. "Oh, what a beautiful piece of material," she exclaimed.

"You like it?"

"Oh, yes, it's beautiful," she replied, but then a shadow fell on her little face. "Does Daddy like it?"

It was my turn to show anxiety. Before I could reply, she said, "Oh, Mummy, you didn't show him! Why didn't you show him? I know you were afraid he would quarrel. Oh, Mummy, if you had shown him, he would have quarreled already and tonight you would go to the party. But now you will show him tonight. He will quarrel tonight and you won't be able to go to the party. You will have to stay home."

It happened exactly as Erica predicted. This tiny little girl could predict the arguments even before they came about.

In the presence of my children, family, friends, and even strangers, I was constantly humiliated, demeaned, and mortified. Lio would criticize the food, the furniture, everything. Nothing was right. Nothing would suit him. The more I tried, the more I failed, and the more deprecating were the remarks that assailed me.

The time came when my friends and family would no longer visit me in my home. My father, after spending time with us in San Fernando, said to Mama, "Never again will I go to that house and endure that tension. I do not understand that man."

Baby continued to visit me and offered me great support and comfort.

"I come here only to see my sister and my nieces," she announced to Lionel. "I don't care how badly you behave. I choose to ignore it for the privilege of being with my sister and these babies."

I went with the girls every month to Arima to spend a weekend with my family. Lio would drop us off and pick us up. At the end of one of those visits I and the girls were at my parents' home waiting for him to pick us up. A friend up the street rang and asked me to come over. I told my family to tell Lio that he could pick me up at the friend's house—"Tell him to just honk and I will be there." When Lio stopped by and heard I wasn't home, he said, "Dammit, she can stay," and took the children home. I was just four houses away. He had to pass in front of the house anyway. But he left me there.

When I heard what he had done I said, "I can't believe he has done this, I can't believe he has done this." The next day I drove out to San Fernando, picked up the children, and took them back to Arima. I decided I was not going back, ever. But three months later I was back. My parents didn't encourage me to stay away. They were good to me, but they wanted me to go back to Lio. So I went back.

After this second separation Lio ran into trouble with his colleagues at the government hospital. He was a high caliber professional—the master surgeon of the country told him, "You have the hands of an artist"—but he was impatient with people. He quarreled with everyone about everything. He decided to go into private practice. We moved away from the government quarters in the hospital compound. Lio set up practice in the front room of our home; the veranda was the waiting room.

When Paula was about four years old, she woke up one night screaming and crying. I ran to her bedroom and picked her up. "What happened?"

"Mommy, I dweamed the whole house was burning. I'm cwying and cwying to see the way it burning so."

"No, no, baby, the house is not burning," I soothed. She had the same dream three times. Dreams are taken seriously in our culture. Fire means trouble. I wondered what on earth was making her dream like that. Lio and I weren't quarreling as much. I was feeling quite content.

One day Lio's sister, Vheda, came up calling, "Babsie, how are you?"

"I am well."

"And how is my brother?"

"He is well."

"Well, I had the strangest dream. I dreamed about a lot of quarreling and fighting."

"As a matter of fact these days we are very quiet," I told her. "I am feeling very contented."

"That's good," she said; "I had this bad dream and I was worried about you."

I wondered, but still I wasn't too troubled. Then I had a dream. I dreamed I was dressed completely in white. White is not a color I wear because it takes too much maintenance—you always have to be washing it to keep it clean. I dreamed I was walking on the street. There was

mud on the side of the road. I tried to walk without getting myself dirty. Then a truck sped by and sprayed me
with black, black mud.

That dream disturbed me. It meant big trouble and embarrassment and shame of some kind. But there was nothing at that point.

Then poison pen letters and anonymous phone calls
reporting Lio's philandering began to come. While he was
on staff at the hospital, it seemed natural that he was
friendly with women there; but after he left and continued these friendships, people thought it was funny.
So they wrote to me. I felt haunted. To this day, when I
open a personal letter with a local postmark, I am
frightened.

When the letters and phone calls started, Lio wouldn't
even let me out of the house. He went wild if I went for a
walk with the children. I didn't have any friends, I wasn't
allowed to go anywhere. Lio's efforts to preserve the family made him try to stop my contact with people who
could gossip about him.

Once I agreed to make a dress for the wife of one of his
friends. I didn't dream he could object to that. He caught
me sewing and told me I had too much time. So he dismissed the maid.

Mrs. Kelly, the girls' kindergarten teacher, lived in a
lovely home behind us. One morning we happened to
greet each other over the back fence.

"Oh, Mrs. McHenry, I'm so embarrassed. Today is my
husband's birthday and I'd forgotten all about it. I haven't
even baked him a cake and I must go to school."

"Why, I'd be happy to bake a cake for you, Mrs. Kelly," I offered.

"Would you really? I know you do such exquisite cake decorating, Mrs. McHenry. If I baked the cake, could you please just ice it for me?"

"I'd be more than happy to ice your cake for Mr. Kelly's birthday."

"Thank you so much, Mrs. McHenry. I'll send the cake over this afternoon with my maid."

At lunch, Lionel and I and the two girls were seated at the dining table when the bell rang. Mrs. Kelly's maid stood at the door with the cake.

"What is that?" demanded Lionel. I explained the situation.

"I thought I told you that I don't want you to do anything for anybody. Send it back."

"Why, Lio, I don't think I'd know how to do that."

"Then I'll take it back."

"Please, Lio." I knelt on the floor next to his chair, weeping. "Please, Lio, if you will just let me do this one thing, I promise you I will never undertake anything for anybody again." I would do almost anything to keep the peace. But I struggled with the humiliation my daughters would experience at school in seeing their mother disappoint their teacher; and I struggled with my own shame at failing to help my neighbor.

"Very well, then," he conceded. "I believe you may have learned your lesson this time."

Another day a woman friend of his was visiting and Paula was whining.

"I want a drink," she whined. I got her a drink.

"I want a biscuit." I got her a biscuit.

"I don't want a biscuit," she wailed.

"You want a little discipline, young lady," I responded and gave her two swats on her bottom. She screamed at the indignity of being corrected.

Lionel came up from his patients to see what all the commotion was about. When I explained what happened, he grabbed me by the throat and struck me.

"Don't you ever hit my babies again!" he ordered.

"These are *our* babies and I intend to discipline our children," I retorted. The lady friend sat watching the entire humiliating spectacle. My life of confusion, shame, and torment was becoming unmanageable.

11

Divorce

A woman always knows when her husband is involved with another woman. I knew that Lio was falling into one adulterous relationship after another. I would confront him with one affair and help him get out; then he would fall into another.

There was a girl, a weepy kind of person, who didn't have a mother; so I was mother to her. I took her in, ate with her, sewed clothes for her, dressed her up for dates. Later I found out the dates were with my husband.

At the same time Lio was having an affair with the woman at the grocery store. On Thursday afternoons Lionel served a clinic in a neighboring town; afterwards he and the woman would go out together. I stopped at the grocery store one Thursday and asked the woman not to meet my husband that day as I would be going to speak with him. She telephoned Lionel at the clinic to warn him of my visit. He was waiting for me in a rage. When I got out of the taxicab and began to ascend the front steps, he flew out of his office and began to beat me, hurling me over a banister.

The next day I went to see our family physician.

"Babsie, you must leave this man immediately," the doctor ordered.

"I can't. Where would I go and who would testify for me?"

"I will testify on your behalf. Here is the name of an attorney. Go now."

I didn't want divorce. I was not going to expose the children to that. But I eventually realized that enduring the hardships of my marriage myself was one thing. Subjecting Erica and Paula to the chaos in our home was another.

I gathered a few things and told the girls that we would be going to Grandma and Grandpa's without Daddy. Erica appeared in just a few minutes with slippers on her feet, a little red beret on her head, and her cloth doll in her hands.

"I'm ready to go," she said.

"Don't you want to take your things with you?"

"Uh, uh," she replied. "I only want my Suzie."

I returned once again to my childhood home. I had experienced nearly eight years of repeated adultery, physical abuse, and emotional torment. My mother suggested that perhaps I needed more grace.

"I don't want grace," I told her. "I want out."

The day after I left Lionel, the grocery store woman moved in with him. I later learned that Lionel had been taking her to visit his mother and friends while he was married to me, and no one had ever attempted to correct him.

In spite of everything, I only wanted a separation. Lionel insisted on a divorce. He told the attorney that he would pay for the girls' education, but that he wouldn't give me a penny. Which was fine with me. I didn't want money. I only wanted peace.

The judge awarded the divorce in the summer of 1952 and decreed that Lionel pay $100 a month for life for our support. Lionel honored the court order for six months and then fled the country, accepting a position in the United States where British law could not be invoked. I appealed to him to keep the lines of communication open with our children, because they needed to know their father.

I had never failed an examination or a class in school. I was sure I would succeed in marriage, my vocation, the most important venture of my life. Yet here I failed.

Divorce was the ultimate disgrace to bring upon my family. No one in the family had ever been divorced. The gossip, the lies, were unbearable. My best friends behaved like enemies. I was incapable of shielding myself against the falsehoods and misconstruction. I felt like a rat in a trap.

When Papa went to confession to make his Easter duty, the priest refused to give him absolution.

"You are harboring a divorced woman in your home," chastised the priest.

"But, Father, she's my daughter! What do you want me to do? Must I throw her out in the street?"

I honestly thought about suicide. The fear of hell saved me. However bad this life is, I reasoned, hell is worse; and it lasts forever and ever.

Many times I have counselled people in troubled marriages. Sometimes God gives the grace for reconciliation. Other times the marriage is doomed. In every case, though, I have been known to remark that the only thing worse than a terrible marriage is divorce!

12

Single Parenting

I had vowed never to be a single parent. Yet here I was, a single parent, caring for my daughters alone. My anger made me determined to succeed.

I wanted to protect Erica and Paula from the social reproach that would inevitably confront them. Friends suggested that I revert to my maiden name; but I didn't want the children to have to explain why we didn't have a common family name.

I found a job and looked for a home for us. My last brother, Henry, was still living with our parents; I asked him to come live with us once we found new lodgings so he could be a father figure for the girls. He agreed. Mama and Papa were relieved at this proposition—my sister Baby was now married and she and her husband were living with them. Baby was the last daughter at home, and therefore, in our culture, responsible for our parents.

One night while I was still at my parents' home, I had an amazing, vivid dream. I had no doubt that it w prophetic, but I couldn't interpret it. I was walking out of a church. As I descended the steps to the driveway, a long procession passed on the street. I stepped on the curb to allow them to pass and was filled with wonder. How could all this be happening in the church without my knowledge? As they entered the church, I caught sight of a grotto in which stood the Blessed Virgin Mary, our Lady of Grace. I realized she was also looking at the procession. Her eyes were purple with grief and her face was sad and overshadowed.

Moved in the Spirit I said to her, "Oh, Mary, you are sad because they are passing you straight by! Never mind. I will never pass you straight."

She now directed her sad gaze on me as if seeking some confirmation of my promise.

"Smile with me, Mother of God, just one little smile." After a long, searching gaze, she smiled reluctantly, but her eyes did not smile. I then pleaded, "Bless me, Mother of God, will you bless me?" Her eyes then lifted in smile and she raised her hand, from which fell shimmering drops of blood and water.

I woke up then, enraptured by the experience, and stayed awake pondering it for a long time.

In the morning I told Mama my dream. At first she looked puzzled. Then her face lit up and she said, "Child, you've got a big grace. You've got a big, big grace."

"A grace," I said. "What is a grace?"

There was no answer to this. So, like Mary, I just pondered it in my heart. Some weeks after when I came in from work, my mother said to me, "Your godmother was here today. I think she wants to see you. Go and talk to her."

When I met with Nen Ro, she surprised me by offering the house she lived in as a gift. She had heard from my mother that I was planning to set up an independent household. And since she was going blind with glaucoma, she thought it would be a good idea if I would accept the house and make it suitable for us, allowing her to stay with us until her death.

This was an unbelievable grace. My home and baby-sitting problems were solved. I immediately recalled my dream; I considered Nen Ro's offer to be a gift from the Mother of Jesus to me.

I arranged a mortgage easily and we set about to enlarge the house so that we could accommodate Henry, too. After a few months we were established as a household: Nen Ro, Henry, Erica, Paula, and I. In gratitude to our Lady I named the house "Ave Maria House." I had always promised myself that if ever I had a house I would call it "Saint Anthony's Villa," because of my devotion for Saint Anthony, which I had learned from my mother. In the circumstances, though, I could do no less than honor the Mother of God for her great kindness and solicitude for me in my time of need. Once again I had great hope.

My children became my vocation at this point. I placed them in the convent elementary school of my childhood, where my mother, my sisters, and I had attended. Because I left so early for work, Nen Ro saw the girls off to school in the morning. They ate their lunch with Grandma and

Aunt Baby (the school was across the street from their home). In the afternoon they returned to Nen Ro and Uncle Henry to await my homecoming. The family support was incredible, and the girls tried to cooperate in every way they could.

To surround them with the best possible example, care, and protection, I decided that the girls would not go to their friends' homes to play, but rather invite their friends to our home. I was delighted to find that they chose friends who were the children of the friends I had gone to school with. We seemed to be swallowed up in God's love and concern.

Every day I told the girls, "Come straight home after school." One evening I asked them, "How was Grandma today?"

Erica answered, "She was well when we saw her at midday."

"What do you mean, midday? Didn't you pass by to see her this evening?"

"Mommy, you said 'Come straight home!'" I hadn't realized how seriously they had taken my every word.

"Oh, I didn't mean as straight as that! You can stop by in afternoons and say hello and see how she is."

Many an afternoon I would come home and find several children playing with my two girls. They would sew or draw or play together. The unity I had fostered between them made them strong.

At Christmas Erica and Paula wanted to go out singing carols with their friends. "Who will take you out?" I asked them.

"One of the parents of the other children has agreed to take us."

"No, no. You are much too precious to me. If you go out caroling, it will be with me. So if you want to go out caroling, you can invite your friends to join us."

So I took them out caroling. We walked the length and breadth of the town, serenading at the houses of our friends. And then I walked (I didn't own a car) each child back home to her parents' house. Parents became sure that when their children were with mine, they were well looked after.

Inevitably they collected money from their caroling, and they needed to know what to do with it. I directed them to give it to the Church as charity.

At the end of the caroling season, the girls and their friends asked me to start a girl's youth club for them. They said they would call me "Auntie Babsie." It was a formidable proposition. But I remembered how when I was a young woman there was a program on the radio every Sunday hosted by a lady whom all the children called "Auntie Kay." I used to wish that I could make that kind of contribution to the children of the country, and here was my chance. The children named themselves "A-Teens," meaning that they were striving to be first class teens. Their ages ranged from eleven to twenty. Together we drew up rules for the club. The only qualification for entrance was a desire to be a first class teen in character. You had to want to be good, despite who your parents might be or anything else. Before I knew it thirty-two girls had joined "A-Teens."

I spent all my spare time (and I had increasingly less and less—in 1958 I became alderman of Arima Borough Council) making opportunities for my girls to pursue worthwhile activities and entertainment. They never saw a film unless I first saw it. After screening it, I would take them and their friends and cousins. We walked. We took public transport. We went to tea parties, to concerts, to music festivals, shopping. They were involved in debate, drama, and public service. They served at luncheons in the town, parish bazaars, and fund-raising activities such as bingo. I desired, above all things, to teach them a way of life that would serve them all through their lives. I wanted to provide them with a happy childhood as my parents had provided for me, and I didn't want them to feel that they were missing out because of the absence of their father.

I taught them to make clear responses from their own hearts, based on right principles. The nuns told me how happy they were to have the children as pace-setters for the school. I was amazed and ever so glad. (By now the nuns were being called "Sister" instead of "Mother.")

One day there was a problem with one of the girls and Sister asked, "Erica, what would your mother say if you had done a thing like that?"

"Sister, if my mother even thought that I was *thinking* I would like to do something like that, she would punish me!"

Once Paula came home with another request for money from the school. Money was in short supply. In frustration I said, "Where do these nuns think I'm going to come up with this money?"

"Mummy, you are bound in conscience to contribute to the support of your pastors!" responded Paula. Somehow I came up with the twenty-five cents requested.

I saw that the girls had acquired my mind and knew what I expected of them. That freed me from a lot of anxiety.

Although they were a year apart, I had held Erica back so they could be in the same class and be protection for each other. They were studying by this time to earn scholarships to secondary school. Erica won all the prizes in English and art, while Paula captured the math prizes. Paula had a deeply competitive spirit, like her father. Erica had the temperament of an artist. She wrote poetry, painted, and created little works of art.

I tried to preserve Erica and Paula's childhood as long as I could. There would be no straight skirts, no upswept hair, no makeup, no nylon stockings, no dating until they were sixteen.

"How old until we can marry?" Erica asked.

"Well, I hope that you will wait until age twenty-three or twenty-four," I responded.

"Oh, Paulie, Mummy wants us to be old maids!"

As it turned out, Erica waited to marry until she was thirty-five. She wanted to be sure that her marriage would last until death.

The warmth and support of my extended family enhanced my single parenting. We planned parties for the girls at home, and their uncles taught them to dance.

When they were eighteen the club had debutante balls for them. Motherhood brought joy and happiness to me. Despite the disappointments and sorrow of my marriage, God was blessing me with abundant grace.

13

Inordinate Desires of the Heart

As a young divorced woman, I faced the double insult of my husband's rejection and the suspicion of my married women friends. The former openness with which I had been received by my married friends became overshadowed by mistrust. Everyone assumed that I was looking for a man. And so women felt they had to guard their husbands from me. Once a respectable married woman, now I was alone. Social dynamics changed, and the eyes of the public seemed always to be on me with everyone interpreting in their own way each social interaction I had. My brothers and my brother-in-law tried to protect me. But most of the time I felt like I was in prison. I experienced a real sense of insult, which crippled my natural tendency to friendliness. More anonymous letters and more accusations assailed me. It was a time of learning the ways of the world. And most of the time it was a painful lesson.

Husbands that I respected and thought above reproach

now made inappropriate advances toward me, as if they considered they were doing me a favor by offering themselves. They assumed that I was lonely and desperate. I began to wonder if all men were like my former husband. Were they all womanizers?

Internally I experienced self-recrimination and turmoil. Some of my priest friends suggested that I apply for an annulment. But I felt in my conscience that I had no grounds. I assumed full responsibility for my decision to marry, especially in light of my father's serious reservations, which, in the innermost part of my being, I had resisted. I felt I had no cause to advance. As my mother said, I had made my bed, I would have to sleep in it.

A public apology was necessary for the scandal of divorce that I had brought upon the Church, and I took a long time to do it. In those days we thought that the very act of divorce was grounds for excommunication. Finally I made my public apology in the Catholic national newspaper and I was readmitted to the full privileges of the sacraments and participation in Church activities.

Life burdened me. I caught the bus to get to work, worked like a dog, and returned home bone tired to face the children. Day in and day out the same scenario. I struggled to keep my spirits up.

I couldn't help feeling that I deserved better than what life had meted me. I had been a relatively good girl. I had played by the rules. I had worked hard and married as a virgin. I had intended to have a story-book marriage, living happily ever after, until death do us part. I had been robbed.

Deep in my heart I held an aspiration—an inordinate desire, I call it. I wanted to prove that I wasn't a bad woman. I had hope that I would meet someone who would love me for who I was, without expecting to change me in any way. I felt that someday there should be someone who would provide for me the companionship and respectability of a stable married life that I had been denied. I deserved at least this much comfort. Quietly I nurtured the anger in my soul and the secret desire that sprouted from it.

Both of the girls had won scholarships to the best secondary school in the city. I wrote to their father to ask if he would supplement my earnings to provide for their transportation. IIe wrote back, "When you took the children from me, you undertook to provide for all their needs. Don't burden me with your problems." He also wrote to the girls to tell them that I had deprived them of their birthright and social privileges.

By now, 1959, I had been divorced for eight years. In anger and frustration at this new insult I cried out, "Lord, send me someone who will love me just the way I am, for who I am, without questions and recrimination!" A week later I met Tommy Bleasdell.

The next day the person who had introduced me to him called to say that Tommy was going to ask me to marry him. "The moment you entered the room he knew that you were the person he should marry!"

"Did you tell him I am divorced?"

"Yes, he knows."

"Did you tell him I am a Catholic?"

"Yes, he knows. He's divorced and Catholic, too."

I laughed long and hard. The world has more crazy people in it than anyone could dream about, I decided.

The following night she brought him to visit me. We had an evening of laughter and fun. When they left, she promised to return to spend the following day with me. Tommy would drop her off and pick her up, she said. She kept her promise and we had a beautiful day together. When Tommy didn't arrive to pick her up, she left in a taxi.

Right after she left, my doorbell rang, and there was Tommy. I told him that she had left, and he admitted that he had seen her in the taxi.

"Why did you come?" I asked him.

"I want to talk to you alone."

Reluctantly I let him in, explaining that I was very busy and couldn't talk to him for some time. He said he would wait. When I finally rejoined him in the living room he immediately launched into the story of his life and asked me to marry him. I was impressed by his openness. But I wasn't ready for such a serious topic. I had dated a couple of men already, and didn't mind spending time with Tommy; and though I longed for marriage to make my life "perfect," I wasn't ready to take that step. After all, I was divorced. . . .

Six months later, on December 19, 1959, Tommy and I were married in a civil ceremony. We had no guests, no drinks, no festivities. I felt strongly that since we were both ineligible for a Church wedding, we should not draw anyone else into the shadow of our sin. We would bear the consequences alone.

And so I entered into a completely new phase of my life.

I had not prepared my children adequately for this. Tommy had been very kind to the children, taking them to school and picking them up and being considerate to them. That behavior removed a great source of stress for me. But after our marriage Paula cried herself to sleep every night because she was afraid that I would go to hell. Erica, on the other hand, tried to be philosophical and accept the changed circumstances of her relationship with me. I had taught Erica and Paula all the truth and beauty of the Catholic faith as it had been handed down to me, and I had taught them the laws of the Church. But in raising my daughters to be good Catholics, had I forgotten that my actions spoke to them more loudly than my words? I grew concerned that I was giving my children a double message. I had not weighed the ramifications of this non-sacramental alliance.

One small comfort was that as Catholics, Tommy and I prayed and attended Mass together each week, although we knew we couldn't receive the sacraments. We obeyed Church law, not wanting to add sacrilege to our sins. I figured that when you play tennis, you play by the rules of the game. And when you play football, you play by the rules of that sport. I wouldn't wear football cleats on a tennis court, and I wasn't going to approach the table of the Lord in my present situation. Yet how I hungered for

the privilege of receiving our Lord in the Eucharist during these long years!

I tried to make myself inconspicuous by withdrawing
from all Church activity and giving whatever help I could
quietly, through friends.

One evening when I went to pick up the girls at the
convent school, I met an elderly nun who had taught me.

"Mrs. Mack, I hear you have married again," she said.

"Yes, Mother."

"You've got to leave the man!"

"But, Mother, you don't understand . . . "

"I don't need to understand. This is sin. You've got to
leave the man!"

I knew she was right. Secretly I rejoiced at her courage
in speaking the truth to me in love. At every Mass when
we prayed, "O Lord, I am not worthy, speak but the word
and my soul shall be healed," I would pray, "Oh, Lord, I
am not worthy, but I know that someday you will make
me worthy. I don't know how. But do it, Lord. Somehow,
straighten out this mess and make me once again worthy
to receive you." All I could do was wait on God and hope.
I longed for his mercy, and I cried out for it day and night.

Tommy's wife died, freeing him to marry in the Church.
I now bore the additional burden of being the sole ob-
stacle to his full readmission to fellowship within the
Church. I felt responsible for his deprivation.

He did not feel quite the same way about our position.
Whenever he would introduce me as his wife, I would
speak to him quietly afterwards.

"I am not your wife. I am the woman you live with.

If we grow comfortable in sin, God will not be able to extricate us."

In the Political Arena

The English brought Africans to Trinidad as slaves to work on their plantations. When slavery was abolished in 1834, the plantation owners invited East Indians to come do the work. They sailed from India under indenture, with a certificate of identity that would ensure repatriation if they wished to return to India at the end of the time agreed to. But they stayed. And since they don't practice birth control, their numbers swelled; today they make up a third of Trinidad's population. Most of them are merchants, doctors, lawyers, and teachers.

The descendants of the East Indians and the descendants of the Africans have lived together for more than a century in friendship despite cultural, racial, and religious differences. They have inter-mingled and inter-married and shared each other's lives. As a child, some of my best friends were East Indians. With the transition from a British Colony to an Independent nation within the British Commonwealth of Nations, political tensions threatened inter-racial harmony among our people.

I threw myself into the political arena as a candidate for the general elections. In a bid to establish some kind of balance, I joined the East Indian party, thinking that my presence would make a strong statement for racial integration. Countrymen should not destroy each other over race.

Once again I embroiled my family in turmoil. Political mudslinging and threats that my house would be burned moved me to send the children to stay with friends. I had the closest encounter with death I have ever had. The whole experience was awful.

I lost the election. I thought the ordeal was over; but the party decided to sue the government for rigging the election. My name was in the headlines. Once again, bad press! For a second time I had to pick up the pieces in defeat. Again I had sacrificed everything I thought I was. I had gone in with a pure heart. I came out a public spectacle. I couldn't help wondering if God had some special plans for me that required me to grow accustomed to attention.

Coming Clean

A few years after my political nightmare, Erica and Paula left Trinidad for university study abroad—Erica at Dumbarton of Georgetown in Washington, D.C.; Paula at the University of Toronto. Their father had agreed to provide for this part of their education.

I continued to struggle in my life with Tommy. I had tried to immerse myself in Tommy's friendship, acceptance, and unconditional love; instead problems beset me as they had done in my marriage to Lio. Tommy couldn't fulfill my dream.

I began praying the same prayer in Mass every day: "Lord, I am not worthy that you should come to me. But, Lord, you can make me worthy. I don't know how, but please do it, Lord." Finally I knew that if anything was going to happen, I had to make it happen. God wasn't going to untangle me from the situation without my co-operation. I had to take the initiative.

I visited my sister and confided what I was going to do. She asked me if I would be coming back to live in my former house in Arima.

"Oh God, I don't know what to do!" I cried in anguish.

"You don't know what to do? Pray to the Holy Spirit," she suggested and began praying:

O Holy Spirit, Soul of my soul, I adore Thee.
Enlighten, guide, strengthen, and console me;
Tell me what I ought to do and command me to do it.

I interrupted her. "Where did you get that prayer? I want it. Somebody's got to tell me what to do."

She got up, went to her closet, and pulled out a pamphlet that she had received from the Vatican booth at the 1960 New York World's Fair. As she handed me the pamphlet she continued praying:

I promise to be submissive
in everything that Thou shalt ask of me
and to accept all that Thou permittest
to happen to me,
only show me what is Thy will.

I left with a new surge of hope in my heart. I just knew

that God would answer me. I repeated the prayer all the way home and had it committed to memory by the time I arrived there. I considered it a covenant with God.

A few days later, on December 1, 1964, I announced to Tommy that I was leaving so that I could seek readmittance to the sacraments. We had been together five years. Tommy thought that I was crazy, because all my financial assets were tied up in the house we had built together. But I didn't care about our fine new home or lovely furnishings. I told Tommy that he could keep it all: the house, the armoires, the sofas and chairs, everything. I just wanted to reconcile myself to God.

It reminded me of the story of a poor man eating thick soup. When he pulled out his spoon, he found a drowned mouse on it. He picked it up by the tail and asked, "How did you ever get in here? Anyway, clean you have come and clean you shall go." The man licked his soup off the mouse until it was quite clean. Then he tossed the mouse out.

That is how I left Tommy. Clean I had come, and clean I went! I took with me only a diminished self-esteem and heavy financial burdens.

I left as quietly as I had gotten into the marriage. I was now forty-three years old. I would start from the beginning again.

I went back to live with Nen Ro. I went to confession and felt that I had expiated my sin of rebellion. God had granted me a new chance to live. Tommy, too, returned to the Church. He is now deeply involved in lay ministry and is married with two grown daughters. We are friends today.

God had dealt with the inordinate desire of my heart; and I knew once and for all that marriage was not in God's plan for me. He had something else in mind. I remembered my pledge of many years before, my pledge never to marry; I realized that my inordinate desire for love and approval had clouded my memory, enabling me to break my promise not once, but twice!

This experience gave me a wonderful insight into the choice of vocation. I have been able to guide many troubled marriages into safe harbors, and to counsel many people to accept their personal call in spite of inordinate desires. And I have given away thousands of copies of Baby's prayer to the Holy Spirit. I still pray this prayer every day.

14

A Changing Church,
A Changing Life

In 1967 I retired from my job at Shell Oil/Trinidad Ltd. and began to work as a secretary for the Eastern Caribbean Medical Scheme University of the West Indies. On October 12, 1968, my daughter Paula married Titus Olufemi, a Nigerian studying obstetrics in Toronto.

Vatican II came to Trinidad and the Catholic Church began changing on me. The responses of the Mass were now in English instead of Latin. I wasn't sure if this God of ours could understand English—not Caribbean English, anyway. And if God can understand English, why had we been made to learn Latin? New songs replaced our cherished hymns. The priests expected us to turn around right in the middle of the Mass and shake hands with our neighbors. I was brought up in a Church where my mother used to poke me in the back and say, "Look in front of you. Look at the altar. Mind your own business. That's what you are here for." Now I was being told to look around and tell people, "Peace be with you." I couldn't say, "Peace be with you," without feeling hypocritical. "How can the priest expect me to turn around in the middle of Mass and impart the peace of Christ to other parishioners?" I thought. "How can I give away what I don't have? Where do I get peace to give it away?"

I was uncomfortable in this "new" Church. Faithful Catholics all around me grumbled and complained. Nevertheless, the operative word for Catholics is always "obedience." Though it was hard for me, I wanted to obey. So everything the Church said to do I did.

One Sunday in January 1970, I was walking out of Mass at Santa Rosa when Father Sydney Charles (now bishop of Grenada) stopped me. "Babsie, I want you to go on a retreat for me. It will cost twenty dollars. Don't worry about the money, Babsie, I'll pay for it."

So I attended the first cursillo in Trinidad and my first retreat ever—just when I needed it.

I decided to play the retreat entirely by the rules. If it was possible for a person to hear God, then I would listen. I gave myself entirely to the weekend so that God could accomplish something new.

The first night we heard a meditation from *Prayers of Life* by Michel Quoist, a French priest. "You knocked at my heart and I opened the door to you and you came in. And a whole crowd followed you, the blind, the lame, the deaf, men and women from every nation and race kept on coming." Up until this time I thought I had been an open Catholic. I thought I had been generous with my life and my time, but now I could see how much further I had to go.

At the end of the retreat I realized that what I had been offered was the gift of abandonment to God. I had lived for a whole weekend with no say in how I would pass the time. I came out alive—a miracle of grace. I had encountered a God who could look after me without my help for a whole weekend. Somehow I knew that he could look after me for the rest of my life as well.

Relationships with men had not provided me with peace and contentment; but God could provide for all my needs. After all, he knew me all along. He had been with me in my childhood home, in my classroom, in my marriage, in my workplace. He alone knew my inmost thoughts and needs. He alone could fulfill the deepest longing of my heart. The cursillo was my first invitation to a deeper walk with God. I sought to know God more as an adult and to move on in my precious Catholic faith.

My mother died July 6, 1970, the gift of wisdom alive and active in her until her death. A month later my best friend died. She had been staying with me in Nen Ro's home. The morning of her death I told her, "You bathe quickly, I'll fix breakfast." From the kitchen I heard a thud and hurried to the bathroom to check on her. I found her unconscious. My nephew Richard, Henry's son, picked her up while I ran to phone for the doctor. I thought she was in a coma—she looked so pretty, I thought she was asleep. The doctor came and pronounced her dead. Total consternation.

"I've got to get a holiday," I said to myself. "I must get someplace where I can come to terms with what has happened—two people close to me dying one after the other." I was offered a chance to take a trip to England, which I had longed to do for years. Once I was in England I decided to visit some of Europe as well. So the Lord more than honored my cry for a holiday.

When I came back from the holiday, my godmother complained of a pain in her belly. I took her to the hospital. The doctor said she had a mass in her belly the size of a football. He opened her up and then simply sewed her back up. There was nothing he could do. She died in January 1971.

I grieved deeply for these women who had all had a strong influence on me. I didn't know that the Lord was about to lead me to a strange place, and these three— out of love, of course—might have prevented me from this journey.

"O Lord, if the Church is changing and my world is changing, whom can I turn to but you alone?" I prayed. "I must cling to you, dear God."

I set forth on one of the deepest quests for meaning in my life. Hitherto I had said prayers, but with the changes being made because of Vatican II, I needed to pray more than I had ever prayed before. And I felt the need to pray with others. But I was afraid that nobody would listen, and I told God so: "How can I, a laywoman, with the kind of experiences I've had, and everything else, stand up to bear public witness to you?"

A young seminarian whom I barely knew, Harcourt,

called me one day and said, "I want to pray. Will you pray with me?"

Surprised, I asked, "What ever made you call me?"

"I don't know. I just thought that perhaps you would want to pray. I need to pray."

"All right. I'll get you people. I'll give you my house— provided you lead us."

"That will do, but you will have to prepare dinner for me, and you will have to prepare some sandwiches for the people who come because I think an important part of prayer is breaking bread together."

I could have asked where he expected me to get that kind of money, but I did not because I recognized God's answer to my prayers. "Surely, I'll do anything: I'll invite the people, I'll cook the food, I'll make the sandwiches, I'll do anything." I could not even begin to suspect what God would do through our little group—if I had known, I would have become even more afraid than I already was. Instead, my fears left me. "He's a budding priest, and what are priests for except to pray? I am off the hook."

I invited people to our first Thursday night prayer meeting, to come sit in the presence of God and talk to him. "Let's put our prayer books down and pray from our hearts," I urged. "Let's share with God the things that are worrying us. Let's tell him that we think the pope is crazy, the priests have gone mad. Just be honest. If God is real, he will answer us. If he is not, we have nothing to lose." My mood at that time was, "Lord, this is your last chance. You either talk now, or forever hold your peace."

On September 28, 1971, about thirty of us sat down to

pray, sing, and read the Scriptures. We prayed aloud in each other's presence, sharing our fears and anxieties about the Church. We were not used to praying without being led by a priest. Some liked it. And some did not. Some felt the songs were too Protestant. But it seemed better to pray than to grumble. Some of us continued to meet weekly.

After some time Harcourt was called away to attend a special class for his seminary studies, and he asked if I would continue to lead the people in prayer in his absence. It seemed a pity to interrupt our regular time of prayer, so I agreed.

One by one, though, people stopped coming because it was Babsie who was inviting them all. Every Thursday night I used to have to call them. Some still wouldn't come.

One Thursday night I said to God, "You know what, I am not going to call anyone tonight. It's your meeting. If it's not yours, I don't want it. I'm not calling a soul. If you can invite some people, invite them. If not, don't. If you invite no one, you and I will have the meeting by ourselves."

That night at seven o'clock it rained cats and dogs, as only tropical rain can fall. I sat in my usual chair and said, "Well, Lord, I am here. You are here. Do what you can with me."

No sooner had I uttered those words than I heard a car door slam and footsteps. My niece entered the room and said, "Auntie Babsie, no prayer meeting tonight?"

"I'm here. God's here."

"And John's here and I'm here."

We began to pray. God brought thirteen more people that night, all on his own. That night as we worshipped him, the glory of God fell upon us. For the first time God was making us into a group who knew God and who loved one another.

15

A New Immersion

An Irish-American priest, Father James Duffy, came to visit us in April 1972. By now we had been meeting on Thursday evenings for about six months. My sister Baby, a good Catholic, was afraid of what we were doing; but she came that night to pray with us. She had been bedridden for several months, unable to recover from a surgery; but she wasn't going to miss an opportunity to hear a priest talk to us. Several men lifted her out of bed and carried her to my house.

I expected Father to lead the prayers, but he didn't and said nothing. We prayed and we sang as usual. An hour passed and the priest hadn't yet said a word. He sat in the back with his eyes shut. (I found out afterward that he had been discerning the group, praying for all he was worth, seeking the wisdom and guidance of the Holy Spirit.) Finally Baby whispered to me, "I'm very sick. I want to go home."

"But Baby, can't you wait just a little while?"

"Look here, I'm a distraction I'm in so much pain. I want to go home. This priest will not speak tonight. Just take me home." So the men carried her back home.

After Baby left Father Duffy began to speak quietly. "God wanted to heal that woman and no one prayed for her."

My internal response was, "Lord, have mercy! One more mad priest. How does he know what God wants to do?" But because of my upbringing and the respect I had for priests, I kept silent.

Father Duffy continued, "You have let that woman go without praying for her. Who was she?"

"My sister," I replied.

"The united faith in this room will heal that woman. God wanted to heal her. Will you let me use you as proxy for her?"

"Yes, Father, you can do anything." What else could I have said? I dropped to my knees. Father Duffy gathered everyone around me. "Pray for all you are worth for this woman. Never mind me, you keep on praying." Father Duffy laid his hands on my head and my shoulder and instructed others to lay hands on me as well.

Father began to pray. He prayed in a strange language—I knew it wasn't French, Spanish, or Latin, and certainly not English. I thought, "What's going on here?" I opened one eye to peek at him. His face was gleaming. He looked the way I imagine Stephen must have looked when full of the Holy Spirit, he gazed up at heaven and saw the glory of God (cf. Acts 7:55). Or the way Moses looked when he came down from Mount Sinai. Then I thought, "Oh my God, how irreverent could I be?" and I ducked and continued to pray.

Father began to speak to me as if God were speaking. "I have preserved you for this from your tenderest years. Have I not protected you when men would have destroyed you by lies? Have I not watched over you and saved you from the lying tongues of men, and from tiger's teeth that would have destroyed you? Yes, it was I who preserved you unto this hour that you should do a work for me."

By the prophetic word he exercised, Father Duffy addressed a problem that had been with me since Mrs. Prout cursed me. He spoke directly into it, as if he had seen my whole past through the eyes of God. As he spoke, my life passed before my eyes. I saw Mrs. Prout accusing me of lying when I was six. I remembered my father spanking me for the first time. Prior to that, I believed my father loved me too much to spank me. My mother used to beat us all the time, with her slippers, with anything within reach. But my father—I never thought he would spank me, but he did, all because of a lie. I remembered the shame and deceit and hurt of my marriages and all the lies; the poison pen letters and anonymous phone calls; the gossip and the suspicion. The curse had colored my every experience. I had come to the point where I stopped defending myself. People could believe what they wanted to. I felt isolated, like I had no real friends. I knew that in a crunch all my friends would decide against me.

Father Duffy's words to me seemed to enter my very soul. I couldn't believe it. I suddenly realized that God knew me, and all my problems, and all I had been through, and the workings of my heart; and I began to weep. A dam broke loose. I cried like someone was flogging me. I realized that God had looked over and preserved me in the hour of peril all through the years. All the time he had been there during the battle. I cried because I was experiencing the mercy of God, because God said that he loved me, that he saw my tears, that my tears mattered to him.

I felt the curse lift. I said to the Lord in my heart, "Lord, you knew it. You saw it all along. You knew they were lying all along." Just knowing that God had been with me throughout those forty-five years freed me and delivered me from years and years of anguish and pain. "Lord, you knew when they lied, and you loved me still. I have nothing to worry about." I was completely free, amazingly free. So even now when people lie about me and slander me, I remember that God knows me, he loves me, he knows what is true.

Then I turned to the Lord and said, "What is it you want me to do? What is the work you want me to do for you?"

Father Duffy continued: "I love you, my daughter, and I desire that you would do a work for me. Pray all the time. Fast much. I love you, my daughter."

Now, I was the kind of Catholic who would argue about whether ice cream was food or drink so that I could have it on a fast day. And the first word God said to me was "fast much."

"Peace, my daughter," Father said. "I impart to you my

divine peace which passeth all understanding. I give to you the gift of peace, deep and abiding."

In that moment I understood the kiss of peace at Mass and realized that Christians could impart God's gift of peace to one another. My tears dried up, the heaving stopped, and I was filled with peace and joy. Then, as one would stretch out one's hand to a princess, Father Duffy stretched out his hand, lifted me up, and kissed me on the cheek. It was as if Jesus himself had kissed me and set a seal on me. Jesus was the bridegroom and I was the bride. I felt peace and warmth flow through me.

When he finished praying over me, Father Duffy picked up a Bible and read where it fell open:

You have been my helper against my adversaries.
You have saved me from death,
    and kept back my body from the pit,
From the clutches of the nether world you have snatched my feet;
    you have delivered me, in your great mercy,
From the scourge of a slanderous tongue,
    and from lips that went over to falsehood;
From the snare of those who watched for my downfall,
    and from the power of those who sought my life;
From many a danger you have saved me,
    from flames that hemmed me in on every side;
From the midst of unremitting fire,
    from the deep belly of the nether world;
from deceiving lips and painters of lies,
    from the arrows of dishonest tongues.

I was at the point of death,
  my soul was nearing the depths of the nether world;
I turned every way, but there was no one to help me,
  I looked for one to sustain me, but could find no one.
But then I remembered the mercies of the Lord,
  his kindness through ages past (Sir 51:2–8 NAB).

How could he have known the whole story of my life? Peace and joy and laughter welled up in me. The moon was shimmering. The people around me suddenly looked so pretty. Everything was renewed and transformed in an instant. I wanted to jump and shout, sing and dance.

When Father left my friends offered to help with the dishes.

"No, it's okay," I said. "I'll do them later. Let's dance. I just feel like dancing!"

"Babsie, you're crazy!" they laughed, and went home.

I washed dishes until about two in the morning. I still felt like dancing. I went to bed, but I couldn't sleep. My mind tried to sort out what my heart and my spirit were experiencing. I lay awake, basking in the immense love of God for me.

Understanding God's Call

The next morning when I awoke, a joy was beating a paean of praise in my heart. Everything looked different. Everything had changed. I thought, "This priest has bewitched me. I've got to talk to him. What has happened?"

I drove to the presbytery to talk to Father Duffy. I knew that I had changed. I didn't know what had happened, because I had barely heard of the charismatic renewal, but I knew that something big had happened in my life. When I arrived at the presbytery, my heart failed me. "I've never talked to a priest just for my own sake. I've gone to a priest to take messages in emergency situations, but other than that the only thing I've ever said to a priest is 'Yes, Father,' 'No, Father,' or 'Amen.'" I turned the car around and drove right back out of his driveway.

I decided to go check on Baby. When I opened her door, there she was working like mad through the house.

"How are you?"

"Babs, I am afraid."

"Why are you afraid?"

"Well, you know how sick I've been. This morning I woke up with no pain and decided to get out of bed. I bathed and dressed and fixed breakfast for the children. Then I started to sweep and clean. I haven't fixed breakfast for the children in months. Babsie, it's ten o'clock, I've not gone back to bed, and I don't know if I'm sick or if I'm well."

So I asked, "How do you feel?"

"I feel well. No pain at all."

"Why not act as if you are well and you will surely find out if you are sick!"

She answered, "I guess so."

The telephone rang. The maid of the house answered it. "Mrs. Bleasdell, it's for you."

I said, "Not a soul in the world knows where I am."

"Mmm hmm," the maid said. "It sounds like a white priest." *White* priest. How does a white priest sound on the telephone? So I went to find out who the white priest was.

It was Father Duffy. He asked to meet with me.

"How did you know I am here?"

"I am at the rectory and I inquired about you. They told me who you are, and someone saw you go to your sister's house."

I jumped into the car and went back to the presbytery. When I saw him I said, "Father, before you say anything to me, how does one fast much? I am a Catholic who on fast days argues whether ice cream is food or drink. Do you understand?"

"Yes, I understand."

"And as for praying all the time, I guess I know a lot of prayers and I could try, but Father . . ."

"All right Babsie," he interrupted, "I'll say this: When God calls you, he enables you."

Those words shot like a bolt of lightning through my whole being. When God calls you, he enables you. That's what God did for Mary. The angel spoke to her and she said, "How can this be?" For me it was "How can I fast much, I who like food so much? How can I pray all the time when I have so many other things to do?"

Father Duffy explained the gifts of the Holy Spirit and something he called baptism in the Holy Spirit—not a new baptism, not a new sacrament, but a release of the graces given in Baptism and Confirmation. It seemed amazing to me. Yet I had seen my beloved sister well and walking around, working like she hadn't in months. And my own spirit was so peaceful and grateful.

At my Confirmation I was told to make my commitment, I made it, and the bishop laid hands on me. I was told that Confirmation made me a strong and perfect Christian, a soldier of Jesus Christ. "Soldiers are for war," I thought. "What is this war?" As I grew older I became aware that I was running away from the war between good and evil instead of engaging in battle. I lacked something.

At seven I had said the words of commitment in reverence, in wonder, and in awe. The sacrament gave me the gifts of the Holy Spirit; but until this point I had not experienced such an outpouring of their power. Now life took on a completely new, glorious turn. Life became full.

I didn't know that the Holy Spirit was touching the hearts and minds of Christians around the world in similar ways. People spoke of being "born again," or "giving their lives to Christ," or "coming to know Jesus in a personal way," or "being baptized in the Holy Spirit." They were repenting of serious sin, committing their lives to Christ, and enjoying greater freedom in worship. The Scriptures came alive for them. They hungered for preaching and teaching from the Word of God. Praise and worship of God in jubilant songs and strange tongues burst forth from their lips, similar to the accounts of Pentecost in the Acts of the Apostles.

Scripture says that in him we receive new life and are able to say, "I am a new creation." I remember one young person said to me, "I thought that when I received Jesus into my life that my life would become dull and boring."

The enemy has deceived us into thinking that being a Christian is no fun. I discovered that I had never had fun until I met Jesus person to person and gave my life to him. That is when my fun really began.

I realized that God had exercised gifts of prophecy, healing, knowledge, wisdom, and tongues through Father Duffy. So many gifts were released in this one priest that it became clear to me what the Irish nuns had told me as a child: The priest is the living presence of Christ on earth.

16

Responding to God's Call

At work that day and for weeks after I wondered about my prayer-meeting experience. God was calling me to something. I didn't know what it was, or when he would hold me accountable, or how I would accomplish it; but I took comfort in Father Duffy's words: "When God calls you, he enables you." The Holy Spirit waited and worked on me for years, gradually molding me until I could say from the heart, "Yes, Lord, anything that you want." Then he gave me the answer.

And day by day the Lord opened my mind and my heart. I used to wonder, "Can man really know God?" I now knew that I could, deeply and personally. I now saw prayer as a means of conversing with God on an intimate level, as standing in awe before an ever-present God. The words of the psalmists and saints became my own utterance. My heart could sing with Hannah and Mary, "My soul doth magnify the Lord."

The Holy Spirit was reminding me of and bringing to

life things that the Irish nuns had taught me, things that I had set aside in the struggles of my life. Waves of gratitude to the Church and her missionaries surged within me. I made my peace with Vatican II—I saw clearly that it didn't matter how many changes had been made in the outward form of the Church: the eternal remained the same. I experienced a burning desire to pass on to others the heritage I had received and had taken for granted for so long.

One Sunday morning I was serving breakfast to my nephews, Richard, Garth, and Nayland, and another young man named Max, who was a Seventh Day Adventist.

"Who is Jesus to you?" I asked them.

"You mean the man, Christ Jesus, or his principles?" Nayland asked.

"The man, Christ Jesus, of course, not his principles."

Pensively he replied, "I believe his principles, but I don't know the man."

"Then you could as well be a Moslem." I then turned to Max and said, "Who is Jesus to you?"

His clarity and candor stunned me. "He is my life. He is my all."

That night I awakened my next door neighbor, another Seventh Day Adventist, who had been one of my classmates in the public elementary school.

"Irene, who is Jesus to you?" We talked for a long time. It strengthened my resolve to bring Jesus into the center of the heart of anyone who would listen to me. I was discovering a deep bond with those who knew Jesus personally, regardless of their denomination. That was a big surprise to me. Something within me changed, and it became visible to all those who knew me. As Saint Paul says, "We are the aroma of Christ for God among those who are being saved and among those who are perishing, to the latter an odor of death that leads to death, to the former an odor of life that leads to life" (2 Cor 2:15–16 NAB).

A few days later I was talking to an evangelical minister with whom I had developed a good relationship. When he recognized this new zeal within me, he knew that I had experienced what Protestants call "being born again."

Filled with joy he asked, "When are you going to leave the Church?"

"Leave the Church?"

"You know the Catholic Church is the whore of Babylon," he said. "Now that you know the truth of Jesus, you must be baptized and worship with others who know this same truth."

I looked him straight in the eye and asked, "Do you really believe that?"

"Yes."

"Well, I want you to know that I don't believe that. But even if I did I wouldn't leave. I would see that every man Jack was out first."

"I don't understand," he said.

"You think I'm a rat?" I said. "Only rats desert a sinking ship. I have been born among these people. I have lived all my life with them. Do you think I could desert them? If I knew the way to salvation, I would consider it my life's business to stay among them until the last one had come to the same knowledge as I. Have you ever preached in a Catholic Church?"

"No."

"And you never will because you don't love the Church. But I am inside and I love her." I looked to the sky and said, "Lord Jesus Christ, you hear me. If this is true, Lord, I'll be the door. And I won't leave until the last man is out. The Church is the Church! Lord, help me!"

From then on the determination to bring every Catholic into a personal encounter with Jesus in his Church became the goal of my life.

Once, at the end of a particularly exhausting work day, I was being driven home, and next to the driver sat a boy about fifteen years old. The boy was ranting and raving about the audacity of his parents to have chosen a religion for him before he was old enough to choose for himself. He went on and on about how his rights had been infringed upon. I said to myself, "I would like to tell this kid something." Finally I poked my head between the boy and the driver and said, "Too bad your mother didn't wait until you could decide what food you wanted to eat before she fed you."

He whipped his head around and glared at me. "What do you mean?"

I said, "You see, if she had done that, you wouldn't be here. You would've been dead a long time ago and I wouldn't have had to listen to all the stuff you've been talking about."

The boy turned back around and didn't say another word; but I'm sure he was still thinking about what I had said.

For most of us Catholics the choice of baptism is made for us. Through the prayers of our families and the Church, Jesus was invited to come into our lives. When our parents brought us before God and the Church, asking for the grace of baptism, they were imparting the greatest treasure that they had—the treasure of their Faith. Baptism was the greatest favor our parents could have done for us.

I burn with the desire that those who turn to God will never live to reproach him but love him with their whole hearts. I like to say, with Jesus, "I am sent to the lost sheep of the house of Israel" (cf. Mt 15:24).

17

Old Wounds Healed

The walk with God is fraught with the unexpected—I discovered this very early. Late one night, in August 1972, as I lay in bed, the telephone rang.

"Babsie, where is your husband?" asked a male voice from the distant past. It was Terry, Lio's sister's husband, of whom I had many treasured memories of friendship and sympathy.

"My husband? Whom do you mean, the man Christ Jesus?" Twenty years had passed since my divorce from Lio.

"Babsie, I'm serious. I went to the airport tonight to pick up Lio, but I was late and missed the flight. On inquiry I learned that he had arrived in a wheelchair and left in a taxi. I've phoned the major hotels and I can't find him. I'm very worried."

"That's too bad," I said. "I'm sure wherever he is, he's comfortable in some woman's arms. But what does that have to do with me?"

"There are many hotels in your area. You live near the airport. Will you ring some of them for me and see what you can find out?"

"Terry," I said, "for old time's sake, I will do it for you, and I will call you back if I can learn anything." I phoned a few places without success.

"Terry, I've called all the places I could think of for you and got only negative responses. I can't find out anything. I'm going to bed. Good night."

As I lay in bed, I prayed for Lio's safety; though deep in my heart I felt there was nothing to worry about.

The following day, Terry called me again. "Babsie, Lio is with me. He's safe, but he wants to see you."

"Tell him that anything he could possibly want to talk to me about is over twenty one and he can talk to them himself," I said, referring to our daughters.

"No, no, Babsie. He's serious and he wants to see you and you must respond to that."

"Very sorry, no interest."

"Please, Babsie, think this thing over and don't dismiss it so rashly. He needs to see you."

"That would take a lot of thought and prayer."

"Then go and pray," Terry challenged. "I'm sure if you pray God will give you the grace to respond kindly to this."

A million questions stormed my mind. Was God really asking this of me? What good purpose could be served at this point? I kept calling on the Holy Spirit to enlighten and guide me. When Terry called back, I agreed to go to San Fernando and hear Lio out. I took one of my cousins with me and dropped her off with friends when we arrived in San Fernando.

I wasn't prepared for what illness—Lio had had five strokes—had done to this proud man. He sat with his cane close by; and his eyesight was diminished. I greeted him. He reached out his hand toward me. I took it and reached down to kiss him.

Lio spoke. "You came to pick me up. Am I going with you?"

The mistress of the house in which Lio was staying called me aside and explained that Lio deeply needed my indulgence—at my home.

"No, no, that is impossible," I replied firmly.

"Please, Babsie, he really needs time to talk to you. Please consider it and take him home with you."

Compassion urged me to say yes; but moral questions stirred in my being. After all, he was a married man with two children by his current wife. I asked to be excused and left the house, promising to come back. I needed to pray and I needed someone to pray with, someone who understood the ways of God.

I hurried to the home of a young woman with whom I had had a prayer experience. As soon as she opened her door, I blurted, "Look, I need to pray about something right away. You don't know anything about me, but I've been married before and my first husband is here in San Fernando. I've just met him for the first time in many years and he wants me to take him home with me."

"Is he married again?"

"Yes."

"You can't do that."

"I know. I know! But . . ."

"But you want to know God's will?" she finished. "Come." She led me to her bedroom and we knelt by the bed.

She began the simplest prayer I have ever heard. "Father, Babsie wants to know your will. You will never deny knowledge of your will to anyone who sincerely wants to know it. Please, help us." Then, softly, she began to pray in tongues. I joined her in wonder and in awe.

Suddenly she turned to me. "Is there anyone at home who can give you an answer?"

"My cousin is at home, but I've never known him to give a straight answer yet."

"Call him and ask him."

"You don't understand. He's a recovering alcoholic."

"Babsie, will you stop wasting time and make the telephone call?"

"I don't even know if he's at home at this hour . . ."

"Call."

I did as she said, not believing that anything good could come out of this.

"Hello," came my cousin's voice over the line.

"Lenny, Lio wants to come home with me."

"Bring him," he said, without hesitation.

"You don't understand," I began.

"What are you anxious about, the room? I will have it ready by the time you get here."

"Babsie, stop wasting time," my friend interjected. "And do what you have to do." By this time the cousin who had accompanied me to San Fernando had joined us. After I explained my dilemma, she picked up a Bible and asked the Lord to give us a word in our predicament. Then she opened it and read the first words her eyes fell upon: "Jesus said to him, 'What you are going to do, do quickly'" (Jn 13:27 RSVCE). She slammed the Bible shut. At the time I didn't realize these were Jesus' words to Judas at the Last Supper; but I got the message.

My friend blessed me for the journey, and my cousin and I returned to Lio. I found him sitting with his suitcase by his side. He looked up and said, "You've come to get me? You're taking me home with you?" The gentle, childlike question took me completely by surprise and broke down the resistance in my heart. I thanked the mistress of the house. Then we were on our way to Arima.

All the way home, as I tried to make conversation with him, I prayed under my breath. At home the room was ready, as Lenny had promised. Lenny greeted Lio and then split the scene, leaving the two of us alone. I prepared dinner for Lio and asked what he would like to drink.

"Rum and ginger."

By some miracle I had rum and ginger on hand and mixed the drink for him.

"You haven't forgotten, have you?" he complimented.

"I have forgotten nothing," I answered, no compliment intended.

I sat with him as he ate and we tried to make conversation. When it was time to go to bed, I wondered how much help he would need. That soon became apparent. I drew his bath, helped bathe him, dressed him, and settled him. We said night prayers together.

Twenty years ago I would have given everything I owned just to be able to pray with him. Twenty years ago I languished for a compliment when I prepared his meals. Twenty years ago the friendship I yearned for had been impossible. But now he desired it himself. Life is surely an enigma. And so often, so much comes too late.

As I was leaving the room, Lio said, "Will you come and lie down with me?"

"I am not your wife. You are married to another woman. And the last thing I want is another husband."

He smiled and said, "Who is talking about a husband? I'm simply asking you to lie at my side."

"I am not the same person you knew twenty years ago."

"I know it," he said. "I heard you praying under your breath all the way as we drove."

As I looked at him I had a flashback of the night I spent with my brother Sylvester after his exploratory surgery. Waking up from surgery and finding me sitting at his bed, he asked, "Have you been sitting there all night? Come and lie next to me." I objected that the bed was too small for both of us.

"You are my little sister. I can't sleep while you sit there. Come and rest."

For his sake, I lay down with him. Now it seemed the same, only this time it was my little brother who needed me to lie down with him, to be a friend.

He stretched out his arm exactly as he would have done

in the early days of our marriage, and he asked me to rest my head on it. I was afraid because he was so sick. But he insisted that it would be fine. I complied and he began to talk. He asked questions about all that had happened to us since we had left him. He wanted to understand all of the things that had caused our unhappiness. As I related some of the painful memories he kept saying, "I can't believe I did that. How could I have been so wicked?"

After awhile he began to talk about his own life. "I bought a diamond ring for Babsie."

"Listen, I am Babsie. For whom did you buy the diamond ring?"

"I mean Euklin," he said. That was the name of his present wife.

"Have you ever called her Babsie?"

"I have done it all the time. She has lived with it for eighteen years. I have never been married to anyone but you. I have never really loved anyone but you."

How could this be? How could love be so distorted? How could two young people so waste a lifetime? Who had robbed us of what could have been a fruitful relationship? I fell asleep with these questions racing through my mind. We were like two lonely children trying to unravel the cobwebs that had entangled us.

Morning broke. All of the pain of the past seemed to have been healed while I slept. I was beginning to understand unconditional love. My duty was to help him to come to the healing that he sought and then to send him back home to pick up the threads of his own life.

Somehow it now seemed easy and desirable. I felt deep gratitude that the nightmare was over.

He told me that the doctor in America had recommended sunshine and sea baths. I took him to the doctor to be examined, and then I requested a few days' leave from my work to take Lio to the sea to care for him.

My brother Henry came to the house to visit. When he saw Lio, he said a gruff "Good morning." Then he turned around and went to Baby's house, steaming with rage. "Do you know that Lio is in Babsie's house?"

In good old Barnes fashion, she replied, "Who said 'I do,' you or she?"

He left to deal with his own anger; but he finally came back and provided a great support, as did my sister and her husband. In fact, my whole family pulled together to help in the reconciliation.

One day a friend rang me up.

"Babsie, someone told me that she saw you with a crippled person who looked like your husband."

"Yes," I replied. "Lio is here with me."

She burst into tears. "Are you crazy? How could you do that after all that has happened?"

Quietly I said, "Wait. Wait. This is the biggest grace that God has given me. You can't imagine what a joy it is to come to peace with him and put the past to rest. Don't cry. In serving him I've had glimpses of what our life might have been like. He can actually say 'thank you' and pay a compliment for a kindness given. God is doing an amazing thing."

I arranged for Father Duffy to pray with Lio for

healing. Father Duffy was also shocked. He had known nothing about my past. But as a man of God, he responded to the request for prayer and encouraged Lio.

By the end of the month healing was visible. Lio could walk without his cane, and he stopped taking his medication. When I took him to the airport, I got permission to take him onto the plane itself. I fastened his seat belt, feeling that a chapter in my life had closed. All my pain was healed. And all reproach was swallowed up in the sea of God's forgetfulness.

I have often wondered if God would have been able to see us through our difficulties if I had been more mature or if my prayer life at twenty-three had been what it was at fifty-two. My mother had assured me that God would give me more grace. But back then I hadn't wanted grace. I had wanted out.

About a year later Lio's wife came to Trinidad. Terry called me to San Fernando to talk with her. It was a strange meeting. She asked me if I would look after Lio for a month so that she could obtain some medical attention. She cried copiously and asked that her tears be excused.

"I am no stranger to tears," I replied. "It is one thing that I understand very well."

"He has been a good husband," she said.

"That's more than I can say."

"Of course he has never been faithful to me. But he has been a good provider."

What could I say to that? I could have made the same statement twenty years earlier. But she and I had chosen two different responses to the same problem. I agreed to care for him while she attended to her own medical needs.

Lio died some years later. Paula and Erica attended the funeral with their husbands and mourned the loss of their father.

When Lio's will was read, I was deeply saddened to learn that he had left nothing to our daughters. Paula's husband was left some outdated medical books, but the girls received nothing.

From this ordeal I learned that we cannot expect from anyone more than they have to give. What you don't have you cannot give to another. I also learned that the most important call in our lives is ultimately to return to God who created us. Every encounter I have had has been necessary for God to fulfill this primary purpose in my life. And available in every encounter, even the most difficult and painful, is the grace of the Holy Spirit to accomplish God's perfect will.

God tried to save me from unnecessary pain. But because of my own stubbornness or ignorance, I had to pass through the fire. As I grew to understand his mercy and forgiveness, it became simpler to extend that mercy and forgiveness to others. I could extricate the gifts of God from the piles of garbage that I had accumulated as I traveled along. I could shine up the wealth of jewels discovered in the rubble and display them to other travellers whose painful experiences imprison them, stunt their growth, or obstruct their path to freedom and exhilarating new life.

18

Growing in the Spirit

Before 1972 I felt that it would be presumptuous to pray for the extraordinary gifts of the Holy Spirit (prophecy, for example). I had been taught that whatever God wants to give you, he will give you. Take what you get; don't ask for anything. But in studying more deeply the writings of Saint Paul I learned that we should ask for and seek these gifts. I became eager to pray for whatever God wanted to give me.

Once while in prayer I experienced a strong anointing of the Holy Spirit on my head, my hands, my knees, and my feet. Warmth flowed through me, but I had no comprehension of what I was experiencing. Shortly thereafter I was browsing in Bethany Bookstore in Trinidad and picked up a leaflet entitled "The Anointing of a Crusader." It explained that the Holy Spirit anoints the head for wisdom, the hands for healing, the knees flexed for praying, and the feet to run with the good news of the Gospel.

Father Duffy invited me to a prayer meeting in the city

so that he could teach me a few things. He tried to help me discern the movement of the Holy Spirit as we prayed over people. When I saw the effects of his prophetic word on those who heard it, I wished with all my heart that I could appropriate this gift. Looking at him and listening to him made me desire everything that God had to give. As usual, I took some friends along with me. I couldn't bear to receive anything alone. I wanted to share everything God was giving me.

The Gift of Worship

That year (1972) Father Robert DeGrandis came to Trinidad to hold a day of renewal for us. He invited everyone to come up and ask for whatever gifts they wanted. I felt like a midwife as I led the people to the altar rail. As they knelt and asked for gifts, I thought of what I would ask for myself. I ran through the gamut of gifts in the Bible. But every time I thought I had decided on one, I would say, what's the use of that, it will pass away.

Finally my turn came. I knelt at the rail. Father asked, "Babsie, what gift do you want?" Much to my own surprise I answered, "All I want is the gift of worship. Jesus said, 'The Father seeks those who will worship him in spirit and truth.'" Father gave me a look I will never forget. Then he laid his hands on me and prayed for what I had asked.

I still feel that there is much to be desired in this

respect. I continue to sigh to God, "Give me the gift to worship you with all my heart and all my soul and all my strength." I am convinced that when this gift is perfected in me there is nothing that the Father will deny me if I ask it in Jesus' name.

The Renewal Spreads through Trinidad

Harcourt returned to pick up where he had left off, but a strange thing happened. Every time we began to pray or plan together, we wound up arguing. Finally I asked, "Harcourt, what's wrong with you? Why is this happening?"

"I don't know, Auntie Babsie. I don't know why I am doing this. I don't want to act like this."

Frustrated, we continued our work, and we continued our petty squabbles.

One day Harcourt came for the prayer meeting and shared with me that he had been illuminated while he was praying in the seminary garden. He thought that he must have been baptized in the Holy Spirit, although he had not prayed in tongues.

Later that evening we were praying over a woman and Harcourt prayed aloud, "Lord, give Margaret the gift of tongues. She is worthy to receive it. Please, Lord, let her have it." At that moment he burst into tongues. Harcourt and I rediscovered the peace and friendship that we had enjoyed. He later remarked that the probable cause of our contention was that God had baptized me in his

Holy Spirit first, and so we had been viewing things with different eyes.

Harcourt was invited to start a prayer meeting at Saint Charles Parish nearby. We began as a team in a private home, giving birth to a thriving prayer group, "Eternal Light." Some of those people came also to our Arima prayer meeting. Other parish priests around the island invited us to come to their parishes and begin prayer meetings. We embarked upon a busy life! Phones rang incessantly. Sleep was an elusive treasure as deep in the night I found myself returning home from various parts of the country.

When priests would invite me to their parishes to found prayer groups, I would say, "You have people from your parish coming to my prayer group. They will be able to start it."

"No, no," they would say. "I will wait until you come. You love the Church. I will entrust my flock to you. If the people don't love the Church they will draw the flock to other congregations."

From my home we became responsible for thirteen prayer groups. All the leaders would meet every Monday night and learn from tapes and books by international leaders in the charismatic renewal, like Ralph Martin. Then we would prepare the teaching for the prayer groups.

Harcourt once again left to continue his seminary training. It took courage to decide to carry on with the prayer meetings by myself. I felt I could not afford to be up in front. The old feeling of unworthiness haunted me. I rehearsed in my own mind all of the reproaches that could

be hurled upon me. "You are a divorcée! Who are you to
lead people in prayer? You have been a source of scandal
in the Church. How dare you?" But I knew that I could
not deny God what he was asking. I had said no to him
too many times in my life and I wasn't going to do it again.

The renewal was spreading in Trinidad, reminiscent
of Psalm 80:8–11 (NJB):

> You brought a vine out of Egypt
> to plant it you drove out nations;
> you cleared a space for it,
> it took root and filled the whole country.
> The mountains were covered with its shade,
> and the cedars of God with its branches,
> its boughs stretched as far as the sea,
> its shoots as far as the River.

People began to flood my house on prayer meeting
night until they overflowed into the bedrooms and the
kitchen; they spilled out onto the veranda, into the yard,
and into the street. They sat on windowsills, tables, and
the floor. One evening a priest came to say Mass for us
and then left quickly, unable to understand what was
going on. I called to my young cousin Terry to play his
guitar for us, but he never responded. At the end of the
evening I spotted him.

"Terry, where were you? I was calling and calling."

With tears in his eyes he said, "Auntie Babsie, I was
hearing you, but I couldn't get to you through the crowd.
I was trapped in the kitchen amidst a crowd of people I

didn't know. I kept asking them to let me pass, but nobody would move to let me come." He lamented, "They have taken our thing from us."

"It's not our thing, it's God's thing." I began to worry about what had overtaken us. With the house overflowing I realized that we could not continue in the privacy of my home. I hesitantly approached the principal of Holy Cross Catholic College for permission to use the chapel, which could hold five hundred people.

"Father, you know we've been having a prayer meeting in my house?"

"Yes, Babsie, I know," Father Foley answered.

"Father, the house is overflowing and we cannot continue to meet here."

There was silence on the other end of the phone.

"Father, we want to ask you if you would permit us to use your chapel."

"Yes, Babsie."

"Can we have it, Father?"

To my shock he said, "Yes, Babsie."

"Could we use it tonight, Father?"

"Yes, Babsie."

Now our great challenge was getting the people up the hill to the college. We had many elderly; and I wasn't even sure the young ones would want to trek up the hill. I made my car available to taxi people up to the chapel. I stood at my gate to announce the change of location and ask those who arrived by car to carry others up the hill. Most people, even many of the elderly, still chose to walk.

When I got to the chapel there was a teeming mass of

people gathered, filling every chair. The young people were singing. Joy filled the place. But my heart failed me at the sight of the crowd. Then I noticed an Irish Dominican priest leading his people out of a bus into the chapel. How could I stand in front of this priest and lead the people in Scripture reading and prayer? I began to weep, angry at God for putting me in this position. I cried to the Lord, "Shucks, Man, I didn't ask for all this!"

A voice seemed to answer, "What did you really ask for?"

"Nothing. I just wanted to know the truth."

Silence.

A peace seemed to swallow me up and I said, "Okay, Jesus. It's you and me. I have nothing to lose. My reputation has been ruined and you know it. But your reputation is at stake. You'll have to defend yourself." I dried my eyes and headed in, determined to avoid eye contact with this priest, whoever he was.

The meeting was joy-filled, faith-filled, hope-filled, prayer-filled. In our culture we don't have baby-sitters, so there were babies and children and teenagers amidst the adults and elderly; there were rich and poor, black and white. God's people had come from everywhere to pray together—and the most surprised person was me!

The Gift of Teaching

During one of Father Duffy's visits, I arranged for a weekend retreat for leaders. I borrowed the Holy Ghost building (the building the Spiritans were using as a junior seminary). I worked head over heels for this retreat, feeling that if I wanted things done, I would have to do them. I put Father Duffy up in the seminary residence and ran back and forth getting meals to him. I started all night worship of the Blessed Sacrament.

I had agreed to give a talk during the retreat; but when the time came for me to deliver this talk I had nothing prepared. I panicked. "Lord," I prayed, "you have to help. I'm going to open this book and speak on whatever comes up." My Bible fell to John 4, the story of the Samaritan woman at the well. I read the passage to the people, then began to speak. I heard myself saying things I had never said or heard before, or even thought about. I felt like I was a flute that someone was playing. I spoke like this for a full hour.

At the end of the talk the priests and lay people expressed their amazement at the wisdom that had been revealed. I was as amazed as everyone else. I knew that God had rescued me from embarrassment.

The duties of the retreat kept me busy late into the night. At two-thirty I tumbled into bed, utterly exhausted.

An hour later I awakened, full of energy. I felt totally alive, every particle of my flesh pulsating with life. I heard the Lord say, "Babsie, I want you to teach my people."

Startled, I responded, "Me, Lord? Teach? But I don't know anything to teach."

"Never mind. I will teach you and you will teach them." Immediately he gave me my first teaching. By a vision he showed me people laying their hands on other people for the baptism of the Holy Spirit. I muttered, "Father Claude wouldn't buy that at all." Father Claude Montes de Oca was our unofficial liaison with the archbishop. He was a very nice, very holy man, but extremely careful about Church doctrine—he guarded the Church like a bulldog.

The Lord said—and this was a clear, clear conversation, not just an awareness in my heart—the Lord said, "If this is the way I choose to impart my spirit, will you do it just because I say so? Yield, man, yield!" In that instant I understood what the Protestants mean when they say "yield" and what the Catholics mean when they say "offer it up." I understood what my mother meant when she said, "A la volunte de Dieu." So my first teaching following this conversation was on what it means to yield and come into acceptance. It was the first thing I ever taught because for the first time I understood it myself.

I began to ask the Lord, "Teach me about this, teach me about that. Holy Spirit, Jesus said when you came you would teach us all things and lead us into all truth. Jesus, you promised that the Spirit would teach me. Please help me, teach me that I may teach others." Then in a vision I would learn a teaching. I would learn things—know them as if through infused knowledge—as if I had studied them. And then the Lord would lead me to a book where it could be confirmed, or to some teacher who would tell me about it. So I knew for sure that the Lord had called me to the charism of teaching.

I always relate this charism to Mary's Annunciation. God asked her to have a child, she said she couldn't, the angel said the Holy Spirit would come upon her, and she yielded. Well, the Lord calls each of us; and he enables us to obey his call by the same overshadowing of the Holy Spirit, in which we receive the power of the Most High.

In April 1973 I experienced a vision of the Blessed Mother. As I reflected on Mary's role, the mystery of free will became so clear to me. I also recalled my earlier dream some twenty years ago in which a procession of people was passing the Blessed Mother straight by on its way to church. Suddenly I wondered if Catholics in the charismatic renewal would be coming to Jesus, but not including Mary on their way. It saddened me, for Jesus had given us his mother to love and to keep.

The Gift of Prophecy

I used to think that prophets were people who foretold only the future. But the prophetic word, I learned from Saint Paul, lifts up and builds up God's people. The gift of prophecy is the "now" word of God. Every moment God wants to talk to his people. What God says to us now is not necessarily what he will say to us later tonight or what he said to us yesterday. One thing is certain, however: if God says something to me and I have not obeyed, when I come back for another word he will repeat the old word. He will not change his word until we have obeyed the old ones. It's just like a mother getting up in the morning and telling her child to clean his room. Later, she hears, "Mommy, Mommy, can I go to the picnic?" "Have you cleaned your room?" "No, Mommy." "Clean your

We Three

Myself at age 18, brother Henry, and sister Baby. We called ourselves "The Gang."

My courageous brother, Cyril.

My gentle and generous godmother,
Rita (Nen Ro) Lafon.

Dr. and Mrs. Lionel McHenry

O happy day! Myself, Erica and Lio on Erica's baptismal day, October 7, 1945.

A grand celebration: Papa and Mama Barnes' 50th wedding anniversary, June 29, 1951 I'm in the third row from front, third from right. Paula and Erica are in the first row; third and fourth from right.

Bringing up the girls: Paula, Erica, myself and A-Teens, about 1960.

Extending the family: This is Paula and Titus' wedding in Toronto, Canada, 1968.
Fr. Bob Madden, myself, Titus, Paula, Erica, Charles Omole.

My first gift of conversion was Cursillo, January 1970. I'm third from right in the back row.

Responding to God's call to teach His people. Early 1980's.

The family tree grew even more at Erica's wedding on June 29, 1980—Erica, myself and Alan.

I like to teach with illustrations. In 1990 at the National Catholic Charismatic Leaders Conference I explain our need to open our eyes to what God is doing in our midst.

Speaking at Franciscan University of Steubenville, 1991.

Fr. Michael Moses is my eldest spiritual son. We enjoy sharing the "the Joy of the Lord" with others. Early 1990's.

His holiness, John Paul II greets me after the International Priests' Retreat in Rome, 1992. He is truly my good shepherd.

In 1994 my good friend Fr. Harold Cohen, SJ, and I share how special we all are as God's children. This photo was taken during a pilgrimage to Israel where I explored my spiritual roots.

God has given me a heart for his beloved priests. My favorite conference at Franciscan Univeristy is the Priests' Conference. This is in 1992.

This picture from 1995 shows my distant family member Brother George Etienne, of Mt. St. Benedict Monestary in Tunapuna. He used to call me "da queen." He recently passed on to his eternal reward.

Housemother Chrysanta takes good care of the children at the House of Grace, 1995.

Chrysanta and I are helping Lawrence, one of our special children, 1995.

With Deborah DeRosia in front of the new Catholic Charismatic
Renewal Center in Caroni, Trinidad, in 1995.

Daily Mass at Ave Maria House. Mr. Bailey, age 98, is to the left of
the pillar.

Myself and Laurie Watson Manhardt on a Marian pilgrimage in France, 1995.

The Joy of the Lord, 1997.

room." Five hours later, "What are we having for dinner?"
"Have you cleaned your room?" A good mother doesn't
go any further until the child has obeyed. It's the same
way with God.

The Lord said to me, "You will never come to me for a
word and leave without it. I promise you, whenever you
seek me for a word, I will give it to you. You can count on
me for that." I knew then that he held me responsible for
the charism of prophetic insight.

Prophecy is one lending one's tongue and voice to God,
and God speaking through the prophet. When I am praying and listening for the word of God, most of the time
he will give me a symbol. If God shows me a fox, for instance, right away I might begin to think of Herod who is
referred to in Scripture as a fox, a man who is deceitful,
cunning. Then I ask God, "What are you telling me? What
do you want me to say?" I know that since a fox is cunning, God might be trying to warn against someone who
is deceitful, perhaps the cunning of false teachers. And I
begin to prophesy, and my first phrase is "The Lord says";
and it's like pulling the first Kleenex out of the box. When
you pull the first one, what happens? There's another one
right there. So I say, "The Lord says, I will warn you of
those who are false in your midst if you will believe in
me," and the next phrase is there, and the next. The
prophecy is born on my tongue: it bypasses my mind.
The Lord says, "Open your mouth and I will fill it." I don't
sit down at home and have an inspiration and come to
the prayer meeting that night to give that word, because
that was the word for two o'clock. Prophecy is the "now"

word of God. It must be born in the prayer meeting, right there.

I have heard it said many times—from the pulpit, by friends—God doesn't come with a noise; God comes in a wee small voice. My response is, "Then try to help me understand Pentecost." We can't limit God. We can't tie down God. God comes like a gentle breeze, as to Elijah. He comes in tongues of fire, as at Pentecost. He comes any way he wants to come. There is no way we can predict how he will come to each of us, but we can be sure that whatever he says will be in accordance with Scripture.

My life has been deeply affected by the prophetic word. I am so anxious to hear what God has to say that if a mouse squeaks in the quiet time, I listen, because there is no limit to the ways in which God may choose to speak to me.

My friends gathered one day to pray, and one of their children, a four-year-old girl, didn't want to pray but to play. When the time came to listen for a word from God, the little child, through tears, squeaked, "The Lord says, 'I do not like you at all.'" We know that God would never say that, but rather, "I love you with an everlasting love." She was projecting her own little feelings of anger toward her parents for making her stay and pray.

Early in the renewal, a friend wrote to me from England that she had been praying for me and the Lord had given her an image and a word. It was so real to her, she even drew what she saw. She saw me in a room praying, then in a stadium before many people, addressing them. The Lord told her, "I will send her out to the nations. I will have her take my word to countries everywhere. . . ." Upon reading my friend's letter, I thought, "Poor little me from this little town of Arima. God will send me out. . . ." I didn't think the prophecy meant anything, but I saved her letter. Ten years later, I was thumbing through my Bible and came across that letter. The prophecy contained therein had been fulfilled word for word.

I feel most responsible for the charisms of teaching and prophecy. Every other gift that I have exercised—the charism of evangelist, the charism of apostle, the charisms of healing and deliverance—all flow out of the teaching ministry and prophetic insight.

The Gift of Healing

At the prayer meetings when we prayed with each other amazing things happened. One Sunday I served at a prayer group in San Rafael. A grandmother approached me with a child. "Auntie Babsie, I want you to pray with this child. She is six years old and she has never spoken." The emotion that I experienced was panic. I said to myself, "What does she think I am, God? I don't want to pray for this." But then I looked at the grandmother's face. She was so simple and so intent that I didn't want to hurt her faith. So I turned and silently said to God, "Lord, she has faith to pray for this child. And I don't have it.

But I remember what you did for the young boy who was deaf and dumb. If that was good enough for you, it will have to be good enough for me." I laid my hands on the child's ear. "In the name of Jesus, be now open." Then I placed my hands on the vocal chords. I spoke to the vocal chords in the name of Jesus, asking the precious Blood to wash these chords and enervate them. I spoke to the nerves in the ear, asking Jesus to do the same thing by the power of his Blood. And then I prayed a little in the Spirit and thanked Jesus for his healing power.

The next thought I had was, "You had better get out of here before they ask you to raise the dead." And I literally ran.

The following Sunday I went back to the meeting, and the grandmother brought the child. She said, "The child spoke, you know." I wanted to blurt, "Oh, Jesus, I don't believe!" I put my hand to my mouth and said, "When did she speak?"

"Thursday" (four days after I had prayed with her).

"What did she say?"

"She said 'Jesus.' We can't shut her up. She is talking incessantly."

"Praise God!" I said.

By the next year the girl had covered all the work she would have done if she had begun school on time. That's one of the things I consider to be spectacular. I say this to encourage people to pray—you never know what God will do.

Another time at a prayer meeting a woman fell ill. I asked some people to pray with her and I continued my teaching. Then someone said, "I am very nervous about the lady who is sick. I feel you should go and pray with her."

"There are other people praying with her," I replied."

"I feel you should be the one praying for her. I am nervous."

So I went to the sick woman. When I got there I found her alone, lying flat on her back on the ground. "Where are the people who were praying for you?" I asked.

"They went to the telephone to get a doctor."

"But this is a prayer meeting and somebody should be praying!" I laid hands on her and began praying. While I was praying she turned completely pale. She broke into a sweat—there was so much sweat that she seemed to be covered in water. I had a sense that she died. Panic seized me. I cried out to God, "No! You can't allow this to happen! Imagine the newspapers tomorrow morning: 'Woman dies at prayer meeting.'" This was at the beginning of the renewal when the renewal was anathema to so many; and this prayer meeting was at an Anglican Church. I said, "Lord, imagine the confusion tomorrow when the newspapers carry this story! Imagine the archbishop's position when he hears that a Catholic woman is carrying on a prayer meeting in an Anglican Church and a woman dies under her hand. You just cannot allow this. For the sake of your own name, Lord, act and bring this woman back to life!"

Then I began to pray more seriously, looking and hoping that someone else would come and help me pray. I saw a young seminarian walking toward me. "O Jesus, Ronnie will help me." But he was walking backwards away from us. I cried out again, "Jesus, I am alone, just you and me! For the sake of your own name, give life to this woman!" Then I said, "In the name of Jesus, I impart life to you now. Come alive, in Jesus' name!"

To my great relief her eyes opened. I said, "How do you feel?"

"All right, but I am very weak."

"God can help that. God can change that." Again laying hands on her I prayed that the strength of God would invigorate her and the life of God would fill her and she would be well.

Her face began to recapture her color. I asked again, "How do you feel now?"

She said with more confidence, "I feel well. But you know how these doctors are. And if the doctor comes and finds me walking around, she will be angry and feel that I wasted her time."

I responded, "Lady, you are all right. God bless you." I immediately closed the meeting and disappeared.

When I caught up with Ronnie some time after, I said to him, "Ronnie, how could you have done that to me? I thought you were coming to help me pray."

"Babsie, when I saw what was happening, I knew that woman was dead. I didn't have the courage to come and help. My thought was, 'Leave her alone. I will only be a drain on her faith. Let God work it out with her.' And as you see, he did."

A Sinner with a Message

As I had feared, people began to gossip about me. I decided to insulate myself. As soon as gossip reached me I would say, "Please tell whoever spoke to you to please come and tell me himself." The burden of adverse criticism and libelous rumors was too great. In order to carry on, I decided that I would preface every talk I gave with the statement that of all sinners, I was the greatest. And I would plead that those who could not bear the sight of me might close their eyes, but not their ears, because I bore a message that was vital to life.

I wanted to say to every person, "God knows you personally. And he loves you with a deep and personal love. And the good news is that whoever you are, Jesus has come to save you."

To the cry "Who is Babsie Bleasdell?" I answer, "Who was Mary Magdalene? And yet her name has been enshrined in the Book of Life. If you think you know bad things about me, I know much more how much I owe to the great mercy of God!"

19

Free for the Lord's Work

Through these early days of the renewal in Trinidad, I continued working as administrative assistant to the dean of the medical college. People started showing up in my office not to see the doctor but to speak with me. One day, of the twelve people in the waiting room, eight of them were waiting for me. This was my workplace, for heaven's sake! How could I deal with all of this? I struggled to keep on top of my job and my work with the prayer meetings. I returned to the office in the evenings and worked until midnight. I worked on Saturdays. I monitored thirteen prayer meetings from my home. I read everything I could find so I could share it with others. I could hardly keep up.

One Saturday I went to the office to attend to some urgent matters. Two of the hospital staff came into the room; one indicated that the other was losing her baby. I telephoned all around the hospital to find the obstetrician, without success. Finally the first woman returned to her work, leaving the expectant woman in my care. Each time I tried to type the woman spoke to me. I gave up on my work and asked the lady, who was Hindu, if she would like me to pray with her. I warned her I only knew how to pray in the name of Jesus, but she nodded her agreement. When I finished praying the doctor arrived. Later the woman brought her husband and family to thank me and tell me that she was sure that her baby was spared at the moment I had prayed with her.

I knew that I had to give something up. The more I wrestled with it, the more I knew that God would win out over my job. But almost everyone that I spoke to tried to convince me that I was being irrational, since I had no money in the bank to fall back on, no other means of support.

In the midst of my turmoil Father Duffy brought a prophetic word: "There is a high way and a low way. And each man must choose the way he will travel. I assure you that if you choose the low way, I will be with you. And if you choose the high way, I will be with you. You would that I would say clearly which way you should choose. But again I say to you, there is a high way and a low way and you must choose, lest when the going gets hard and the way gets dark you will reproach me. My daughter, I assure you I am with you. Choose according to the dictates of your heart."

I wrote a letter of resignation. My boss refused to accept it.

Then I traveled to Canada on a five-week charter to visit Paula and her family. While I was there I attended a prayer meeting in Toronto. Afterward I was invited to go to a charismatic conference at the University of Notre Dame.

It was the most wonderful, breathtaking experience of my life. Here were thousands of people gathered together as if for a festival, and all were greeting one another joyfully, "Praise the Lord, brother!" "Praise the Lord, sister!" It was a foretaste of heaven.

After the conference I returned to Toronto. The leaders of the local prayer group invited me to visit with their core group. One evening I walked into a room and saw someone teaching a small group of people. As she taught she wrote on the blackboard all of the Scripture references. I was speechless. I thought to myself, "I would give my eyetooth to be able to teach like that." When I spoke with the coordinator, he offered me the book *The Life in the Spirit Seminars.* I hugged him and headed home with this prize. Up until that time, we just laid hands on people and prayed over them as we felt led by the Spirit.

I took the book to the prayer meeting, but no one seemed interested. Words will not describe my disappointment. Soon after, however, one of the priests from Saint Joseph Parish, the oldest parish in the country, invited me to attend a Better World retreat and to begin a charismatic prayer group after the retreat. Here was my big chance to do a Life in the Spirit Seminar. I followed the book line by line, word by word.

As the day approached for the laying on of hands, I was filled with anxiety. Suppose, just suppose, God didn't come through. What would I do?

Father Duffy agreed to be with me, to say Mass with us

as we prayed for the baptism in the Holy Spirit. All would be well.

When we got to the parish, we met the new priest, Father Curtain. Father Duffy explained who he was, and I was confident that all would be accomplished. Father Curtain welcomed us and gave us his blessing.

"I assure you that I want all that is good for my parishioners; but I would ask that you do not pray for any extraordinary gifts," he said.

"How does one restrain the Holy Spirit?" I wanted to shout. But I restrained myself as I heard Father Duffy responding, "All right, Father. Thank you very much. We appreciate your welcome and we will respect your wishes."

As we walked away Father Duffy said to me, "Babsie, we will have to postpone the praying over. God is a God of order and he respects the authority that he has set up. I assure you that he will bless and will open the way in the fullness of time for his perfect will. But in the meantime we must respect the authority of the parish priest. The prayer meeting will only thrive as we respect his authority. His blessing is absolutely important, so we must wait."

Fear that I would be alone again when the time came for praying over the people engulfed me. But I submitted to his wisdom.

Soon thereafter the Lord opened for us the way to pray over the people, and all of them came into new life in the Holy Spirit. The archdiocese has been blessed with two beautiful parish priests whose vocations were nurtured by this group. That prayer group still thrives to this day.

Meanwhile I continued to work at the medical college, but I knew I couldn't go on like this forever. I asked God how long he would wait.

One day I met a young pastor from a Pentecostal church. In conversation with him I learned of his own call from a job in public service to the ministry. He explained that one day while he was at a meeting on his knees singing "I Surrender All," he seemed to sense the Lord speaking to him.

"Hypocrite. What have you surrendered for me? What about that job?"

He began to weep. Immediately after the meeting, he wrote a letter of resignation and gave copies to his father and his young wife. He felt that he could not go home until this was done, fearing that he would fail in his resolve to be obedient to God. It had been three years that he had been sensing the need to leave his job, but had taken no action.

"Three years! Would God wait three years?" I asked.

"God's patience is infinite. His gifts and his call are irrevocable."

I was deeply heartened. After all, God hadn't been waiting on me that long. Meeting this young pastor increased my faith that I could do what God was calling me to do despite the discouragement of my friends.

One Saturday evening in December, on my way to Mass, I went out of my way to pick up a family and had an accident. My windscreen was completely shattered. On Monday morning I limped the car down to the repair shop and left it there. When the bill came, it was four dollars less than my salary. I paid it. For the first time in my life I faced a Christmas with no money for gifts and extraordinary preparation. Christmas passed and turned out to be pleasant, despite my strained budget. I was not embarrassed that I had no gifts to give. I enjoyed the extravagance and generosity of all of my friends and family. I was learning humility.

On the last day of the year as I parked my car at the office, I distinctly heard, "This is the last day you are parking this car here with my permission." I jumped. I literally jumped. I knew it was the Lord. I covered my face with my hands and I sighed.

"What do you want me to do, Lord? I have no money in the bank."

"If you can live through Christmas without money, tell me, when can't you?"

I sat motionless for a few minutes. I knew he was right. I made up my mind to extricate myself from secular work.

Nevertheless, it took one more strong warning. I was descending the stairway from the office one afternoon when the Lord arrested me with the words, "I will not wait on you forever, you know."

I pulled back and responded, "What, will you get someone else?"

"No, I'll break you." I had no doubt at all that the Lord was serious.

I ran down the steps two at a time, jumped into my car, and sat there praying to the Holy Spirit for a long time. Then I drove home, knowing that I could delay no longer. The following day, in July 1973, I wrote my resignation. This time, contrary to office procedure, I sent the original to the secretary of the university and the copy to my boss, who was away at a medical conference in Japan. He was furious when he returned, but there was nothing he could do. He did remind me that I had promised that whenever I was leaving I would give him time to recruit a proper replacement. I promised him that I would keep my word, even though the termination date was the end of the current month. I attended work every day for the next three months until October 1973, receiving no pay! Somehow God covered it.

After training my replacement, I said to my boss, "Look, I am out of here. I'm gone. I've given you three months training this girl. Do the best you can with her."

"If you are determined, I'll have to let you go. I don't know how you are going to make out, but don't look to me. I will not be contributing anything."

"You know that I have worked for the last three months without pay. Perhaps you could apply to the bursary for a stipend to cover some part of the three months."

He looked directly at me and said, "You write the letter. I will sign it."

They sent a check for $802 as a gift for the period of time I had worked without pay. I felt like a millionaire. For three months I had learned how to live without earning any money. The Lord had just provided. Now I was convinced of the truth of Father Duffy's words: "Whom the Lord appoints, he anoints."

I went home, free at last.

20

In the Lord's Employ

Immediately I made Thursday a prayer day. People came at ten o'clock for midmorning prayer from the Liturgy of the Hours, followed by a prayer meeting. Thus we prayed in union with the entire Church. People began coming from work to pray with us. After the prayer meeting some stayed for counseling and fellowship. Then it was time for the Thursday evening prayer meeting.

Each day I responded to whatever called for my attention. One day after a holiday I woke up determined to make myself a new dress. I got the material out and laid it on the table. I got no further. I was interrupted continuously by the telephone and visitors dropping in to see me. By the late afternoon I decided to at least get the material cut before the prayer meeting. As I cut the last piece I said triumphantly, "At least I have cut you. I don't care that I haven't sewed anything. The next chance I get, I'll do the sewing. But I've accounted for my day and that's it." The day ended and I went to bed.

At two-thirty in the morning the Lord woke me and said, "So, you tried to take a day off after a public holiday?" I knew it was the Lord. It reminded me so much of my father, who would never permit us to stay home on a Monday or on the day after a holiday, however sick we might be. Papa would say, "Go to work and let the boss see you sick and let him send you home if he wants to. That's his privilege. But, if you stay at home, it could always be said that you were drunk after having too much spare time."

I remained dead still and the Lord continued.

"When you were working, would you have taken a day off after a public holiday?"

"No, Lord."

"Have you lacked anything since you have been working for me?"

"No, Lord."

"Have I been a good task master?"

"Yes, Lord."

"Have I provided for all your needs?"

"Yes, Lord." I was feeling really harried.

Then he said, "When you were at work at your secular job, you were at your desk at eight o'clock every morning. I want you to know that you are now in my employ. You must be dressed every morning by eight o'clock. Don't plan anything on your own, but be open to do whatever I send for you to do."

"Yes, Lord," I said, and spent the rest of the night in prayer. This Lord meant business. I had much to learn about serving him.

It was like tying wild horses to get myself to submit to this discipline. But I prayed the Holy Spirit prayer, not once a day as Cardinal Mercier suggested, but all day long. Gradually I learned to wait on the Lord.

One Friday morning I woke up and found there was nothing to eat in the house. Nothing! I looked around and then said to the Lord. "Well, I don't really need food today. I can make it a day of prayer and fasting. Besides, I can go to my sister and eat with her, or I could drop in at a hundred other houses and have something to eat. So I'll just go and pray." I went to my bedroom and knelt down. I had hardly got into prayer when I heard a call. Going to the door, I saw two little children from families that attended our prayer meetings. Each child had a parcel in her hand. I greeted them and accepted the gifts they had brought. The first bag contained a four-pound frozen chicken and two kilograms of rice. The second contained a coconut and some callaloo leaves—all ingredients for callaloo, a Caribbean soup often served on Sundays in Trinidad. But to prepare this dish one must have okra. I had no okra and I had no money with which to buy some. So I whispered, "Lord, it seems that you want me to cook. But if you do, you know I need okra. If you send them, I promise you that I will cook even though I don't want food."

I put the chicken in the chiller and the other ingredients on the table. In a few moments a friend walked in through the back door, saying, "Babs, I was passing by the market and the okra looked so green and fresh that I couldn't resist them. So I brought you some." She dumped out her package, covering the table with beautiful okra.

After she left, I set about preparing a big Sunday dinner of callaloo even though I had no one to eat it. I had promised God, hadn't I?

About midday as I was turning off the stove, I heard the slam of car doors. I didn't think it had anything to do with me. I wasn't expecting company. I heard the sound of footsteps, followed by the doorbell. When I went to the door, I found six people standing there! They gave a whoop of joy when they found they had come to the right house, and that I was at home. I recognized only one of them from a prayer meeting in San Fernando.

"Hello. What brought you all here? How did you find my house?"

"We were longing to see you," they said, laughing. "We have hunted all over Arima searching for you. And at last we have found you!"

As they entered the house they shrieked, "Oooh, smell this house!" The whole house was filled with the scent of callaloo.

"Babsie," they asked "Is that how you cook on a Friday? We didn't know you could cook."

"Oh, you thought I could only preach?" I joked. "Well, let me tell you, I was a housewife for a hundred years before I became a preacher. Are you hungry?"

"We left home early this morning to find you, and we are dying of hunger."

Soon enough my best china and cutlery were out and we sat down to a sumptuous meal. They licked their fingers, praising God after every morsel. I was picking up the remnants from the table when the doorbell rang again. At the door stood a young man, about sixteen, who had come from a place even farther than San Fernando to find his uncle, who was not at home. He wondered if I could help him with some money to return home. I wanted to help, but I knew I had no money. I spoke to the young man.

"Boy, if your story is true, then you must be hungry."

"Very hungry, Miss."

I sat him down at the table and gave him the remainder of the food. During my working days I had kept a little box of savings. Each day I dropped in a quarter for charity. If I could find that box, I thought, I might be able to provide money for him to return home. I searched, and behold, I found. I was able to send him off rejoicing. My own heart was filled with joy at the awareness that I need not be afraid about the future. God was faithful to his covenant and would provide for me if I lived in obedience to his requests. That day the Lord delivered me from fear and brought me into trust.

21

Faith: Gift and Responsibility

In May 1974, I returned to Notre Dame for a conference, this time with a group from Trinidad. That year we experienced the amazing power of the Lord in healing ministry. I threw myself into the whole experience with total abandonment, praying for all I was worth that God would achieve great exploits; in the midst of it I discovered that my own eyes were completely healed. I had worn spectacles for twenty-five years and had never once thought of praying for healing, because it seemed to me that if you could afford to pay for the spectacles, praying for healing would be superfluous. After the meeting, I returned to the dormitory with my friends. My spectacles were in my pocket and no one noticed that I was without them. Not one person there had known me without them, and yet nobody noticed. At night prayer and morning prayer the next day I actually read without glasses. By the end of the conference, my companions still hadn't noticed.

After the conference the group returned to Trinidad while I went to Toronto to visit Paula. As soon as I walked through her door she shrieked, "Mommy, where are your spectacles? Your eyes have been healed?"

Wanting to downplay it, just in case, I answered, "Well, I think so. But when I can sew without spectacles I'll know for sure."

"That's easy," she said. She went to the clothes cupboard and brought me one of Titus's shirts to alter. "Try this. It should tell you."

On the following day while she was at work, I repaired the shirt. When she returned it was hanging on the rack, fully completed.

She screeched, "Did you do it without your spectacles? Your eyes have really been healed?" She had never seen me without eyeglasses. God was still up to working miracles!

Two days later I was alone in the house getting ready for departure to Trinidad. She had left me the telephone number for a taxi service to take me to the airport. My ticket was nonrefundable. When the moment came for me to make the telephone call, I could find the number nowhere, and there was no one to help me. I remembered the name of the company and tried to find it in the phone book, but I could see nothing, nothing at all. For a moment I panicked. I cried out, "Lord, help me. I know I can see." Nothing happened. I screamed out, "Lord, don't let the devil get me. I know I can see. And even if I can't, I know you can see for me. Let your sight go through my blind eyes." Immediately I saw the number and I dialed.

My chest was heaving; my breath was short. And when the voice on the other side answered, "Able Taxi Service," I almost fainted. I screamed, "That's all right, devil, do your worst. Jesus is Lord." I barely made it to the plane, I had a splitting headache; but I knew once and for all that the enemy would steal from us any gift that the Lord gives. It is our business to hold on in faith in every circumstance.

Beads Bound by Faith

That same year we elected a national service team to oversee the charismatic renewal in Trinidad and Tobago, and I became secretary. In 1975 I was selected to represent the country with Abbot Bernard Vlaar, who was chairman and spiritual director of the team and liaison to the bishop, at the International Leaders' Conference for the Catholic Charismatic Renewal in Rome. There I met with some of the international representatives of the charismatic renewal and really began to understand the scope of what God was doing within the Catholic Church in the world.

At Mass in Saint Peter's Basilica, surrounded by thousands of people singing in tongues, I experienced myself as a bead on a chain. All the beads before me represented the apostles and saints who had gone before, and the beads after me were those to whom I would pass on our faith. The faith was the thread that bound us together. Each bead had to have a hole through which the thread could pass. I saw that faith was both gift and responsibility. Deep gratitude to those who had nurtured me welled up in my heart: my parents, the nuns and priests, my godmother, my teachers in Catholic school. And a deep sense of wonder at the awesome privilege that was given to me in Baptism stirred in me the determination to let nothing deter me from passing on this precious gift. My spirit burned within me, pressing me to get on with the job.

After one of the sessions, Dorothy Ranaghan of the People of Praise in South Bend, Indiana, intercepted me.

"It seems I should know you, but I don't and everybody else does. I'm Dorothy Ranahan."

"I know you from your book, *Catholic Pentecostals*, and I want to thank you for it," I said. "It was my introduction to the Catholic charismatic renewal. Besides, I have seen you at Notre Dame."

"Can you spare a few moments?" Dorothy smiled. "I'd like to ask you a few questions."

She asked about the renewal in the Caribbean and how it was affecting the Church. Altogether we spoke for about five minutes. When I rejoined my friends, they told me that they had seen Dorothy and me on the closed circuit television. It seemed that God wanted to make me visible. I couldn't help wondering what he was up to.

The Power of Expectant Faith

On our return home we began to plan for the first Caribbean Leaders' Conference and National Rally of Prayer

Groups, as we called it. It was a formidable task; but the Sunday in January when we celebrated the Baptism of the Lord, over five thousand lay people, thirty priests, and three Caribbean bishops assembled to praise God.

Because of the great numbers we gathered outside. Black clouds threatened; and just as proceedings were about to begin, the scowling clouds broke and rain came down in torrents. People began to run. I took the microphone and spoke.

"Christians don't run. They stand. God has given us authority over the work of his hands. Let's stand together and command the rain in Jesus' name to cease." They stopped and joined me in prayer. But the torrent increased and the people ran away after all. I found myself standing alone. My spirit failed. I was drenched from head to toe. Water filled my shoes. I turned around, intending to leave, when I beheld three young men of three different races sitting with upturned faces and praying for all they were worth. I gathered courage.

"Lord, you held the sun for Joshua. You can do it for us. You who stilled the waves and the storm can still this storm for the sake of these three young men. For the sake of their faith, I stand in your presence and command these clouds in the name of Jesus be sealed."

In that instant the rain stopped, the clouds parted, and the sun burst forth. The people returned, roaring in triumph. God had shown his favor. The proceedings resumed.

At about midday, the clouds started to gather again and I began to feel discouraged. As I was ascending the stairs to the stage, a man said to me, "That was a wonderful thing you did this morning."

I replied, "But look, what is the use? The clouds threaten again."

He spoke words I will never forget. "Babsie, when God has acted, don't let the symptoms confuse you."

"What do you mean?"

"Didn't you see what God did this morning? Hold on in faith. All is well."

And he was right. For the rest of the day we beheld an amazing spectacle. Rain fell all around us, but not on us. We continued our worship as if we were in a bowl surrounded by a curtain of water. It was a marvelous phenomenon. For me it was a personal endorsement that God honors those who persevere in expectant faith. The sight of the three young men praying with their eyes closed will remain forever a testimony to the courage of youth when they are fired by God.

Men of Color and Men of No Color

In the middle of the last rush for the Caribbean Leaders' Conference, a letter came from Toronto inviting me to take part in their first Ontario Charismatic Conference the following summer. The weight of this decision moved me to push the letter aside and wait for others to help me respond. Later I posted the letter on the bulletin board to see the reaction of the prayer group members. With one voice they urged me to accept the invitation.

I arrived at the conference without any knowledge of what I should do, except that I would share the platform with Father Regimbal, a seven-foot French Canadian priest, who was then coordinator for the Catholic charismatic renewal in eastern Canada. Three thousand expectant, enthusiastic Canadian charismatics gave us a rousing welcome on the opening night. I was surrounded by well-known, strong leaders of the renewal. I felt as conspicuous as a raisin in a sponge cake! And I still did not know what I had to do.

The following day Father Regimbal called me to a meeting, in which I discovered that there were four of us to participate: a Pentecostal pastor, a Jewish woman, Father, and me. I had no clear concept of the part I should play, but I was too shy to ask. I thought I would just wait on the Holy Spirit.

As the meeting progressed a theme emerged of repentance on behalf of Catholics for any offenses or misunderstandings given. But I still had no grasp of my role.

Saturday night, while the four of us were sitting on the stage, Father Regimbal got up and knelt before the Pentecostal pastor and asked his forgiveness for any pain given to Protestants by Catholics. The pastor responded by accepting the apology and offering forgiveness on behalf of his own people. It began to dawn on me that I was probably there as a representative of black people, but I couldn't believe it. I'd had no warning. Then Father knelt at the feet of the Jewish woman and begged her forgiveness as a representative of the Jewish people. And then Father was announcing, "And now, our beautiful black sister from Trinidad will offer forgiveness on behalf of black people for any pain that we may have caused them." He came and knelt at my feet.

Shocked, I opened my mouth. Not a sound came out. He stuck the microphone close to my mouth and said, "Speak into the mike!"

A rush of anger flooded my soul, anger over being asked to be a token black. I heard myself pray, "Father, in your wisdom, you have seen fit to create all things according to your own designs, the flowers of many hues and the birds of the air and the fish of many colors. And all nature has worshipped you. Man, man alone in his arrogance has dared to rebel against you. And now I bow before you in humility and beg your forgiveness on behalf of all men, white men, black men, red men, yellow men, and men of no color. O Lord, we have all sinned against you and against one another, refusing to accept one another as gifts from you. Forgive us, Father and have mercy on us."

I heard sobbing all over the stadium. For a moment I lost all awareness of space or time. Something was happening that I did not understand. People were weeping and sobbing and hugging each another. There was a sprinkling of black people and native Indians who were huddled and being hugged. Suddenly, there was laughing as the joy of repentance filled the whole place. The walls of prejudice seemed to crumble all around us and there was laughter amidst the tears. I stood there in wonder and awe, amazed at what God had done.

Suddenly a native Indian man and wife and children

beckoned me. I went to the edge of the tall stage and knelt to shake his hand, but the man and his wife wanted to kiss me. They were not tall enough to reach the edge of the stage, so I lay down flat on my belly to kiss the man, woman, and children. Cameras flashed, and I was consumed with embarrassment at my prone position on stage in my beautiful clothes. One of the officials tapped me on the shoulder and pointed to the steps that I had overlooked in my confusion. As I came down the steps, I was swarmed by people shaking hands and hugging me. I felt that somehow God had made me a spectacle again. Once again I wondered why. What was he up to?

Years later, I stood outside of a church in Vancouver, British Columbia, waiting for a friend. Becoming a little anxious about whether I was in the right place, I sought help from a passerby. Wide-eyed he said, "Are you by any chance Ursula Bleasdell?"

I nodded in surprise. "How do you know me?"

"I heard you at the Toronto Conference. You called me a man of no color!"

22

Yes, Jesus Is Lord

My sister and I were good friends. I came into this life in the Spirit before she did and I tried to tell her about it. One day she blasted me. She almost turned the car over she was so angry. She said, "Look, you think you know God better than I do, well let me tell you, I've known God from the time I was a young girl. . . ."

Baby was an excellent Catholic. She knew all the fine print in the little catechism, and she could tell you everything the pope said and the pope did, and all that. But back then I knew she hadn't broken through to that place where she really accepted the lordship of Jesus Christ. That day I decided, since I had only one sister, "We are not going to quarrel," and I shut my mouth.

One day she came to our meeting to be prayed over. It just so happened that it was my turn to lead the proceedings and I thought, "Oh, no, if I go in there, she's not going to receive it. Just my presence will be a hindrance to the grace that God wants to give her." So I ran to a friend who was scheduled to lead worship and prayer at the same time and pleaded, "Look, I cannot go in there. For my sister's sake, I cannot go in there. You go in and let me take your tour of duty out here."

My friend went in my stead, and I prayed like anything. When Baby came out I could not ask her, "How did it go? Did you pray in tongues? Did you receive any other gifts? What happened?" even though I was dying to ask her every one of these questions and luxuriate in her detailed answers. I thought, "If I open this big mouth of mine, that will be the end of it. I've got to wait." Sometimes the things we want to see and know most, God does not allow us to see and know, and that's one way he humbles us and trims off all the excess pride. He whittles us down to the size at which he can use us like a powerful sword.

One day I heard Baby's children complain, "Listen, all this preaching you suddenly . . ." and I thought, "She's got it!" but I said nothing.

A short time later she rang me up and said, "Do you know something?"

And I said, "What? I hope it's good news."

She said, "Jesus Christ is Lord!"

And I just said, "What's new?"

"Nothing, but Jesus Christ is Lord."

So I said, "Praise God!" I wanted to add, "I'm glad you found out," but thought better of it. (God's still working on this sword.) "No, no, no," I said to myself, "I can't say that. Many people confess with their lips, but they don't believe in their hearts. I've got to wait, and I've got to be very nice all the time."

Then I added, "That's good. Yes, yes, Jesus Christ is Lord. I know that."

Baby's test from God came soon thereafter, the day of her daughter's wedding. She and her husband had paid a lot of money to rent a posh outdoor reception site because they wanted their daughter to have a beautiful wedding. Well, it poured and poured. Rain fell like it was the time of Noah revisited. Trembling, I asked Baby, "What are you going to do?"

She replied, "Jesus Christ is Lord."

I said, "Yes, Jesus Christ is Lord."

"God will not make me ashamed in the sight of unbelievers."

"Well, I'm glad you believe that."

We went down to decorate and the wind picked up everything and blew it away. It was two o'clock and it was pouring. The wedding reception was scheduled for four o'clock. We cleaned up everything, and I said to Baby, "You know what?"

She cut me off with, "But it's got to stop. It's not four o'clock yet."

I thought, "Boy, Jesus Christ is really Lord in her heart."

So I told Baby, "You go to the wedding Mass. I'll stay here and when the rain stops, I'll put the place in order." And everyone left for the wedding.

At 2:10 the rain came down even harder, the wind roared, lightning flashed, and thunder rolled. I kept talking to the rain because God says, "Speak. I give you authority over the work of my hands." And I said to the clouds, "In the name of Jesus, be sealed." And, "Hey, spirit of the storm, you know you are finished; you know you are beaten. Stop it, in Jesus' name! I'm not taking you on because I know that it's finished." As I said that, the sun came out and smiled.

When the wedding party and family and friends arrived after the wedding, they could not believe the transformation. The sun shone and the sky was clear. We had a wonderful time. Everything went well because Baby knew that Jesus Christ is Lord.

23

Praising God for Babies and Shingles

God seemed to have a hidden agenda for every activity in which I became involved. He made time and resources available in the most amazing ways in almost every family crisis. For instance, when my first grandchild, Olu Kemi (Yoruba for "God has blessed us") was born in Toronto, my cousin gave me an airline ticket as a gift.

Six years later, Paula called me from Bathhurst, New Brunswick, pregnant and sick. "Mummy, I am in hospital. My blood pressure is so high that the baby is in danger and I have to stay in a dark room, under constant medical care. Kemi is alone at home with Titus and I am in this strange new place. I need help."

Paula and Titus had moved to Bathhurst in 1977, when Titus became the head of the obstetrics and gynecology department at Bathhurst Hospital.

"Okay, baby, I'm coming," I responded.

To be truthful, I didn't know at all how this would happen. I didn't even know where Bathhurst was and

I didn't have any money to travel. But within two days God provided both time and money and I was on my way. Willing hands assumed the responsibilities of the prayer community and the airfare was provided in a miraculous way. Surely he is Jehovah Jireh, the Lord who provides.

I was soon at Paula's side, mothering my granddaughter, washing clothes, cooking meals, and telling stories. God was drawing upon the experience that I had acquired in my years as a single parent. In addition I was friend and counselor to my son-in-law, Titus, with whom I spent many pleasant hours of conversation. As an obstetrician he experienced such deep helplessness in the care of his own wife and child that one day, when I tried to talk about God, he cried out, "What does he want, dammit?"

"He wants you! God is meeting you on your own turf and beating you. We can do nothing but pray."

On a day when Paula felt better, she told me there was a prayer meeting in Bathhurst. We went to find it.

"I think they meet in that little chapel right there," Paula said.

"Well, stop and let me inquire."

"I'm sure this is the prayer group."

"Well, how do you know, Paula?"

"See all the people coming out of the chapel, and look at their smiling faces. Can't you tell those are Hallelujah people like you, Mummy?"

Some of the people approached the car.

"Babsie Bleasdell, what are you doing in Bathhurst?" a man asked.

"How do you know me?"

"We heard you in Toronto!" they chorused. "What are you doing in Bathhurst? Have you come to speak to us today?"

"It's okay, Mummy," Paula said. "I'm only concerned about how you will get back home. What time should I come for her?"

"Oh, no, you don't have to worry. We'll bring her back home," they assured her.

So for the next six weeks I attended their prayer meetings. Sometimes they invited me to teach.

Thank God, Olu Kola ("God has increased our riches") Paul was born healthy, though sedated from all the drugs that had to be administered to Paula. After the delivery Paula's obstetrician said to her, "Paula, another pregnancy will cost you your life. You cannot afford to have another child."

One morning after Kola's birth, I awoke with pain under my arm. Two days later the pain was so severe that I looked in the mirror to see if I could locate the source of it. A red rash started under my arm and extended to my back. The doctor diagnosed it as shingles and prescribed a lotion.

"Lord, I came here to help, not to add to burdens," I cried. "Please let your health flow through me." I kept speaking to the shingles, "In the name of Jesus, dry up."

My new friends from the prayer group in Bathhurst visited me to help. These white women applied my medicine to my back. I felt self-conscious, even as I chuckled over the people God chose to send.

In Trinidad I washed clothes by hand, but Paula had a washing machine and vacuum cleaner and everything. A workman came to service the washing machine and left the hose detached. Not suspecting any calamity, I threw in a batch of wash—and flooded the entire basement. I immediately set to work bailing. To drown out the pain of my shingles I praised God at the top of my lungs.

Little Kemi, wanting to ask me for a cookie, found me bailing in the basement. "Grandma, what are you praising God for that for?" she asked, hands on her hips, eyes shooting fire.

"Because he's my only help and I have no one else to call on. And I know he will help me!"

She continued to watch in disbelief, giving up all hope for a cookie. When Titus came home in the evening, he expressed his sorrow and informed me that I could have called in a company who would have brought equipment to suck up the water. Oh, ignorance is bliss!

Four months later Paula telephoned me in Trinidad.

"Mummy, I'm pregnant."

Detecting the anxiety in her voice, I tried to comfort her, saying, "Let God's will be done."

"But the doctors warned me that I couldn't afford another pregnancy."

"Paula, the doctors don't have the last word. God does. We will pray and put it in the hands of God." I trusted God and Paula's deep abiding faith.

As it turned out, Olu Kunle ("God has filled our house") Patrick turned out to be her easiest pregnancy and her liveliest baby.

24

Rungs in the Ladder of Faith

Mary Goddard, a Canadian Pentecostal evangelist and teacher from British Columbia, was propelled into my life at a time when the renewal in Trinidad urgently needed solid teaching on the power and gifts of the Holy Spirit.

Mary came to us from British Columbia via Malaysia and Singapore, with recommendations from the bishops. She lived in my house during her visit—no other Catholic was brave enough to publicly offer hospitality to this white Pentecostal. Mary spent eight weeks in Trinidad and some of the surrounding islands holding teaching seminars. Signs and wonders followed her preaching of the Word of God. As we traveled from town to town and island to island, we bonded in a deep and personal friendship that persists to this day.

Once when we were stranded in a small airport, my back went out. Mary insisted on carrying my bags for me. I led the way, teasing her, "Mary, God has turned the tables on us. One hundred years ago I would have been your slave. You would have walked in front and I would have followed carrying your bags!" We laughed together.

Another time we were having a prayer meeting at the cathedral. A woman came to me with her twelve-year-old child. The child was screaming like crazy. The woman said to me, "I want you to pray with this child for me. She doesn't speak."

I really was afraid. I said to her, "Why do you pick on me? Why don't you go to Mary and ask her?"

"No, I want you to pray." So, moving on the feeling that God would not be pleased if I refused to pray, I reluctantly laid hands on the child and prayed for her. Finally the screaming subsided. I left the country the following day, so I got no news about this lady or her child.

Two months later I went to the cathedral for morning Mass and decided to stay after to do my morning prayers. While I was praying, a lady came to me. In my heart I was feeling, "Gee, whiz, I can never get a quiet place! What on earth does she want?" When I looked up, the lady said, "Do you remember me?" When I told her I wasn't sure, she explained, "I am the lady who asked you to pray with the dumb girl the day there was the big meeting here."

"What happened to her?"

"The child has been speaking. I have a gift that I want to give to you."

I was overwhelmed, astonished. God had done it

again. I assured this lady that I was so grateful for God's kindness that I was already paid and I didn't expect anything from her. But she found my house and brought me a set of bed linens as a gift of appreciation.

I often met her and her child at church festivals. Every time, the child would call out, "Babsie! Babsie!" and I would say in my heart, "Yes. You have the right to call me Babsie. I was afraid to pray. But God healed you with my halting prayers. So although everybody else says 'Auntie Babsie,' you can say 'Babsie.'"

Caribbean Service Team

In 1978 we geared up for a big Caribbean conference. Father Tom Forrest visited with us and we elected the first Caribbean service team, including Father James Duffy (chairman), Father Harcourt Blackett (my young seminarian friend, now a priest) from Barbados, Rose Hall from Grenada, Father Michael Kosack from the U. S. Virgin Islands, Cuthbert Mejias from Trinidad, and me. Father Tom Forrest exhorted us to be faithful to our commitment to the service team.

"You are bound to attend every meeting, except for "grave personal reasons," and grave personal reasons doesn't mean the death or sickness of a close personal relative. It means your own!"

I froze, but I got the message. And for as many years as I served on the team, I never missed a meeting.

Leaders' Conference in Ireland

Some of the men involved in the Caribbean renewal began to complain that women were too predominant in the renewal leadership. So when I was invited to attend the Second International Leaders' Conference in Dublin, Ireland, I declined in favor of sending men from Trinidad with Father Duffy. But because of our close bonds with Ireland—after all, Irish priests and nuns had given birth to and nurtured the Catholic faith within us—about twenty-six other people wanted to attend the conference on their own. Their ages ranged from mid twenties to eighty-four. As I looked at the list, I realized that there was no one to take responsibility for this group; some of the group had never traveled in their lives. They had never ridden elevators or escalators or been on an airplane. They needed a shepherd. My heart really ached to help them, but I didn't have the money for the trip.

A week before the departure date an acquaintance from the prayer meeting came to my house on her way to church. She handed me an envelope, saying, "I don't know why the Lord told me to give you this. But you must have use for it." And she turned and walked away.

When I opened it, I found a check for $1,000.

Two hours later, two younger women dropped in. I had been praying with one of them for her friend to be healed of cancer.

"Babsie," she said, "I wanted to tell you that my friend, for whom you prayed, has gone into remission. And we want to thank you for your prayers, and I brought you a little gift." She handed me a check for $200. Her companion, joining in the act of thanksgiving, gave me two $20 notes. Here I was with $1,240 completely unsolicited. The airfare was $1,239. There was a $2 departure tax. So, by investing $1 of my own, I was able to go. I took this as my confirmation that God wanted me to go and shepherd this group. But his purpose, as usual, reached far beyond that.

Ireland, with its forty shades of green, and its churches, and religious habits everywhere, was a tremendous gift to me. Coming to Ireland was like coming home. Irish priests had baptized us, Irish nuns had taught and nurtured us, and Irish priests had ministered the sacraments to us from birth to death. We could almost hear ourselves singing "Hail, Glorious Saint Patrick" at the top of our lungs while waving little green flags all over again. Hearing the Irish brogue intoxicated me. I constantly had to suppress the desire to sing and dance to the Irish tunes I had heard all my life.

At the last minute, the French contingent scheduled to present an evangelization workshop cancelled. Father Duffy was asked to fill this slot. He called us together to discuss our options. He felt that it would be inappropriate to accept this honor when there were thirty native Caribbean people present.

"I think that Babsie would be the best person to make the presentation," Father Duffy proposed.

"I beg your pardon," I interjected. "There are five Caribbean leaders who came as bona fide representatives here among us and if you do not feel it is appropriate for you to do this, then one of them should. But I think that you are the best person to do this. You are the person who has nurtured Catholic charismatic renewal in the Caribbean and brought us to the place we are."

"No. I am Irish-American. I live and work in the Caribbean, but I am Irish-American. A Caribbean person must do this." He was resolute, even though our whole group tried to persuade him. Finally he said, "Babsie will do it and that's it."

"I will not," I said, and spoke no more.

After our night prayer Father Duffy reminded me that I was due to speak at nine o'clock the following morning.

"No," I said. "I have nothing to tell the Irish people, except thanks for giving us their sons and daughters for so many generations. Nothing. Nothing."

"Then tell them that," he snapped with a finality that silenced me completely.

I made my way to bed with an extremely heavy heart. Sitting by the side of the bed I prayed, "Lord, you see my predicament. I have not sought this. I don't want it. I don't know how I got myself into this. I have nothing to say. And I don't want to say it. But it seems that I have to do it. So I'm asking you to help me, if you can. I'm reminding you that when I stand there in the morning, if I can't open my mouth, your reputation will be at stake. My own reputation was shot long ago. So I have nothing to lose; but you, Lord, you! I would hate to bring dishonor to your Name. Therefore, for the sake of your own Name, I am asking your help. Now I am going to bed."

I awoke in the morning, filled with sheer terror. I said, "Lord, I have nothing that I want to say to the Irish but thank you. If you have anything else that you want me to say, speak now or forever hold your peace. I'm going to open the Scriptures and see whether in your goodness you will give me a word."

I opened the Bible to the Psalms:

It is good to give thanks to the LORD,
    to sing praise to your name, Most High,
To proclaim your kindness at dawn
    and your faithfulness throughout the night
    (92:1-2 NAB).

Let no one think that my prayer was born out of rudeness. It was purely out of terror.

Finally the time came. Three thousand people gathered together to hear the West Indians talk about evangelization. Father Duffy presented our group and led us in singing a Caribbean "Gloria" that captivated the assembly with its calypso rhythm. He introduced himself and described his role among us. Then he presented me.

My breath caught in my throat. Then with a great burst of emotion, I declared that whatever I was, was a result of Irish missionary enterprise. I recounted the sacrificial love with which missionaries of many lands had come to our country. I thanked them all for our education through the schools they had established for toddlers through university level. I thanked them for the Catholic faith they had planted so deeply in our hearts. I thanked Irish mothers for releasing their sons and daughters for the sake of the kingdom. I thanked Irish brothers and sisters for their unselfishness, for their love of God and the Blessed Virgin Mary. I continued to elaborate on their achievements among foreign peoples. It was a tremendous act of thanksgiving that flowed from the depths of my soul.

Once again I beheld the strange phenomenon of people weeping, as if they had become aware for the first time of the privilege that God had afforded them as a people. It was as if the pain of centuries was flowing out of them in an act of thanksgiving to the God who had called and enabled them to do this work.

To worm my way out of the stadium was a Herculean task as Irish mothers and fathers, priests and nuns crowded to thank me for the tribute that I had paid to them as a people. One eighty-year-old Irish nun said to me, "Child, today you made my whole life worthwhile. I had been thinking that my life had been spent in vain." An old Irish missionary priest emotionally thanked me. Irish mothers, sisters, and aunts all wanted to share a warm embrace in thanksgiving for their participation in mission, even though they had stayed at home.

Since 1978, I have hardly tread on foreign ground without being asked, "Were you at the Irish Conference in 1978?" When I nod in acknowledgment, they say something like, "I knew I heard you there. I couldn't miss that voice." The Irish conference was a firm rung in the ladder of my faith.

Pilgrimage to Lourdes and England

After the conference was over, I wanted to do something with the Caribbean people to enshrine the Irish experience in their memories forever. An opportunity to pilgrimage to Lourdes presented itself and we grabbed it. The richness of our tradition and the generosity of a Church that could embrace both the traditional and the charismatic enfolded them as they renewed their baptismal vows in the waters of Lourdes.

A visit to London completed our pilgrimage. In London we enjoyed our political heritage. After all, we were a British colony until 1962, and we parted from Great Britain without hard feelings. We enjoyed boating on the Thames and gazing upon Buckingham Palace and watching the changing of the guard. At the railway and tube stations I had more fun than a picnic as I stayed back and watched each of my novice travelers ascend the escalators. One time I said to the last one, "Now," and stepped on, completely convinced that she would step on with me. She didn't. I looked back just in time to see her disappear in a mass of people. I shouted, "Don't worry, I'm coming back!" I reached the top and took the down escalator, laughing all the way. I felt loudmouthed and visible, but I began to understand the price of mission and the heart of a pioneer. Each time we had to get on a train was an exercise in ingenuity, charity, and hilarity.

Back in Trinidad we celebrated. In a formal dinner we shared our experiences, photographs, and stories in an attempt to cement the bonds that had been formed, not only as Catholics and charismatics, but also as nationals. Although we live together and share a common faith, there was a certain undercurrent of division due to our multiracial and multi-cultural roots. God was breaking down walls—this time in our own backyard.

Word of Life Prayer Community

By the end of 1978, the prayer groups had grown and spread all over the country. We were being called to the Dutch Islands and the British Caribbean Islands to teach and to foster renewal. People were needed to serve these people of God. It became clear that we couldn't continue to serve the groups that were springing up unless we could bind ourselves together. Thus the Word of Life Prayer Community was formally established under the authority of our Archbishop Anthony Pantin. In May 1980 the archbishop celebrated Mass with representatives from all the priestly orders serving our country: Benedictines, Dominicans, Holy Ghost Fathers, and diocesan priests. Along with the Sisters of Saint Joseph of Cluny and Dominican, Carmelite, and Holy Faith sisters, we lay people crowded into the Church of the Holy Spirit in Arima to publicly commit for a year to the Word of Life Prayer Community and to offer our blessings.

The name of the community emerged from the personal unstinted prayer of an exclaustrated abbot of the Cistercian Order, Father Gerald Hawkins, whose religious name was Dom Colamban. He lived in the community with us for a year. Dom Colomban was an Australian by birth and his dream for Christian lay community drove him to the "ends of the earth" in a relentless quest. The Catholic charismatic renewal was a source of great hope to him. He finally arrived in Trinidad from the United States of America, via the Island of Grenada. Dom Colomban initiated our unbroken tradition of a daily midday Mass in the community house. He was also a great inspiration and help to us in the planning of Trinidad's very first C.C.R. Leaders' Conference and National Rally.

One day he emerged from his prayer time glowing as he announced what he thought was God's revelation for the name of our covenant community. He held out the Bible and pointed to Philippians 2:14–16: "Do all that has to be done without complaining or arguing and then you will be innocent and genuine, perfect children of God among a deceitful and underhand brood, and you will shine in the world like bright stars because you are offering it THE WORD OF LIFE." That sealed it for us.

The Lord himself confirmed the choice of our name in his own unique way. I was going through a particularly dark spiritual tunnel when in the travail of my soul I had many searching questions, the chief being, "Why did I ever call the house 'Ave Maria'?"

At that time we were building an extension to accommodate the growing population. In my agony I cried out to God, "The last thing I ever thought I would be doing at this time was sinking money in laying down stone. I don't need all this! Why, O God, am I doing it?" I was walking through the unfinished building when this anguished cry exploded from my lips. As I was passing under the main cross beams, the Spirit of the Lord fell upon me. I felt a large mass of "bridal veil" fall gently on my head. It began to unfurl and wrap itself around me as a voice said clearly, "This house has been called 'Ave Maria' so that it might become the 'Womb of Mary,' bringing forth Christ. Nurture him to full stature and give him away to the whole world."

An inexpressible joy broke over me and I danced with wild abandon, like David before the Ark, crying out, "Lord, if you want it, you can have it. It's all for you!"

I firmly beleive that this prophecy will be fulfilled in God's own timing. In the meantime, I hold on to the vision in faith for the "the just man walks by faith."

25

Mission to Africa

Mary Goddard invited me to go on mission with her to Israel, Greece, and Africa in 1979. I had shared my people with her, and now she was going to share her ministry with me.

In Benin City, Nigeria, I had the privilege of working with Dr. Benson Idahosa, author of *Fire in His Bones*. I taught at his Bible school, where I met many former Catholics. I shared with them the things that God was doing in his Church. Many of them became homesick for Holy Mother Church.

In Nigeria I got my first real taste of mission work and the demands it could make on body, soul, mind, and spirit. Our group was suffering from diarrhea because of the strange food and water. On top of this, a water shortage limited us to flushing the toilet once a day.

I found it so hard that one day on my knees I cried out, "My God, what am I doing here? I want to go home. Get me out of this place."

In the middle of my lamentation the Lord's presence arrested me. "Oh, you weep! You took a plane and came in great pomp to this country, where the climate is like yours and the people look just like you. And now you weep because the food is different and you have a little diarrhea. I see. Can you imagine what it was for me to leave the glory of heaven and come to live with the likes of you?"

My heart dissolved in the presence of a holy God. "Then help me," I cried. This cry to the Lord at last is what I should have done first. As I rose from my knees, I was inspired to take over the cooking. Our stomachs might then be less taxed. I noticed a large papaya tree just outside the door and prepared sliced papaya in cream sauce. The following day we were healed. It took me five years to realize that the pectin in the papaya was God's provision for dealing with our digestive predicament.

The Claim of the River God

While in Africa we were praying with first-generation Christians who had all been pagans and then had given their lives to Christ. One young woman told us, "Whenever I pray, I feel as if things are moving inside of me, and my abdomen really hurts. I am not at peace." I was present when a priest prayed with her for deliverence. She vomited, and in the vomit there were living river creatures. Then she told us that she had been committed to the god of the river as an infant.

People from some Protestant denominations attack the

Catholic Church because they claim that one must be totally immersed in order for baptism to occur, and Catholics only sprinkle. There was a time in my life when this
claim that Catholics are not baptized concerned me. That
changed after this event in Africa. I felt thanksgiving to
God for showing me the claim of the spirit of the river on
this girl. She was not free until she was delivered. If the
god of the river would receive this girl and seal her with
an indelible mark, how much more would the God of
glory receive the child that my parents offered, and mark
me with a seal of baptism.

The Church teaches that while water is necessary matter for baptism, the amount of water used is immaterial.
Water is a symbol of the Holy Spirit and the cleansing of
the soul. The first Christians to be baptized were immersed in water, but over time, especially with the baptism of infants becoming common, pouring water over
the individual during baptism became an accepted practice. When the gospel began to spread to the desert, where
there is no river for hundreds of miles and water is scarce,
baptism by pouring rather than immersion might well
have been the only option for new believers. When Saint
Paul was imprisoned and the jailer converted, there was
no river or pool available, yet Paul still baptized him. And
what of a person on his death bed who receives Jesus?
Would we pick up a person with pneumonia and take him
to a river fifty miles away to dunk him?

Jesus promised the Church that he would be with her
always. And he vested the Church with authority to alter
practices (such as pouring versus immersion in baptism)

as long as the essentials remain (baptizing "in the Name of the Father, and of the Son, and of the Holy Spirit," and the use of water). I believe that I was baptized as a child and that the seed of God was planted in the little mound of flesh that I was. When I was carried into the church, I was a child of nature—Mama's child and Papa's child. Through the prayers of the Church and the consent of my parents, God gave me his Spirit and I became a child of God.

Death of Sylvester

Before our mission ended I received a letter from home telling me that my brother Sylvester had passed on one week after I had left home. This news took two weeks to reach me, long after Sylvester had been buried. Efforts to telephone were futile and three cables were lost in transmission. This brother of mine, whom I always called "my brother who was my father," was gone, and I could not share in the intimate family grief over his passing. Sylvester was like Jesus in that he was the intermediary between my father and us, saving us from Papa's wrath, pleading for us when a thrashing was due. He bridged the gap; he was always there to comfort and console us. He was fun and laughter when everything was glum. A life pulsated from him in which everyone shared. Now my dear Sylvester was gone.

In the moment I received that letter, my heart went out to every missionary in the world who receives sad news from families far away and cannot be with them to grieve with them. I knew that I owed missionaries a debt of gratitude that I could never repay. I thanked God for Jesus who cancels all our debts. I slumped into a chair and wept silently.

The group gathered around me and laid hands on me and prayed silently, until the waves of grief subsided in the peace that only Jesus brings. That same day I left on my return journey home.

26

The Old Rugged Cross

A three-page cable arrived for me from South Bend, Indiana, inviting me to speak in front of twenty-five thousand people at the 1981 Notre Dame Conference. I posted it on the notice board. People would stop and read it.

"Hello! What's happening here?" asked a priest. "You're going to say 'Yes' to this of course."

"No."

"You can't turn that down."

"Oh, yes I can."

"Wow! You can't afford to ignore this," said another. To everyone it was a singular honor to speak at Notre Dame, and each made his own positive comments. A follow-up cable and the egging on of the community convinced me to agree to give a thirty-minute witness.

On a Friday night we gathered for the opening of the Notre Dame Conference. I found myself on stage with Father Harold Cohen and Father (now Bishop) Sam Jacobs. Bill Beatty, who was leading the ceremonies, stepped over to me and asked, "Babsie, do you know 'The Old Rugged Cross'?"

"Yes," I replied.

"Will you do it for me, Babsie?"

I said, "No, no, I can't sing."

"Will you do it for Jesus?"

I remembered my promise and muttered, "I promised God never to say no to him again." I said it out of the grief of my heart. I was doomed.

When the fateful time arrived, Bill came back to me and said, "Are you ready now, dear?"

"No. As a matter of fact, since you asked me I can't remember a single word of it."

"Then I'll pray for you," he whispered. He returned to the mike and announced, "Now our beautiful black sister from Trinidad, Babsie Bleasdell, will sing 'The Old Rugged Cross.'"

I had to do it. But first I said to God, "When I told you I'd never say no to you again, I didn't think that you could be so stupid! You know I can't sing. Now you can take what you get!" As I stepped toward the microphone, sick with fear, I kept whispering, "Lord, hide me, hide me. Twenty-five thousand white people and I am like a raisin in a sponge cake. How could you do such a thing to me?"

The musicians prepared to accompany me. But the key that I started in has never been written or sung before. In despair the musicians one by one put down their instruments. I pressed on, with some members of the audience trying to support me in vain. I sang the first verse to the end, then stopped. I thought the world had come to its end. But the sympathetic crowd erupted in thunderous applause.

I stumbled back to my seat, thinking, "This is ridiculous. Once again I'm a spectacle." I felt that I had experienced the deepest humiliation of my life. It was bad enough they had asked me to speak; but now they had asked me to sing before I could speak. The prospect of facing this crowd again tomorrow was a nightmare. All night long I agonized. I begged the Lord to blot out the memory or use my stupidity in some way to glorify his name. Finally I said, "Lord, I'd give it to you if you could use it. You used the mess of the cross, perhaps you can use my foolishness. Take this mess and do what you want with it. I just want it out of my mind."

The following day, as I was walking toward the stadium, Sister Ann Shields fell in step with me and said, "Babsie, I want to talk to you."

I thought, "What an honor! This great nun wants to talk to me, puny me."

She said, "About last night . . ."

"Sister, for God's sake, not last night. Talk about anything but last night. Last night was easily the worst moment of my life, and I don't want to remember it."

"No, but I want to tell you something."

"Tell me, tell me. I will listen to you."

"As I watched you there, struggling to be obedient, I thought, 'She's doing this just for God. She, an ordinary lay person, is so surrendered to God that she could do that for him. I, a nun, have not surrendered like that. I must do better.' I knew deep down in my heart that I had never surrendered completely to the Lord, and I made a decision to do so."

I said, "Sister, that's what it did for you?"

"That's what it did for me."

"Praise God! I asked him to glorify his name and save souls. That's okay. I don't have any more burdens. He has taken my pain."

If we give God our pain, he will take it, purify it, bless it, and use it for the honor and glory of his name and to save souls. I don't hold on to my pain because God can use it.

As if God wanted to make up for the excruciating humiliation of that night, he empowered me to give a talk that moved many hearts. I recounted a simple event in my family. For years my daughter Erica had creamed butter and sugar by hand for all the cakes we made. She was always ready to offer her strong little hands for this service. Then one day I bought an electric mixer, thinking that I would relieve her of this burden. On the night we set it up, she disappeared into her room, and I had to invite her twice before she would come see it work. Within a few minutes the machine completed its job. She got up from the table without a word and started to leave.

"Where are you going?" I asked her.

She replied, eyes full of tears, "You don't need me. You have that thing!"

What should have been a moment of triumph turned into a moment of sadness. My daughter, who had served me so happily, now felt useless, rejected, cast aside. Immediately I realized that people were more important to me than things. And then I drew a parallel between that and what could possibly be an American response to God. Becoming more and more dependent on things, we become less and less aware of our need for one another and less and less dependent on God. And as we become richer in material things, we can become poorer in character because of our alienation from God.

I closed the talk with Proverbs 31, on the ideal woman.

She is clothed with strength and dignity,
    and she laughs at the days to come (Prv 31:25 NAB).

To my great shock, the conference committee sold over a thousand tapes of my talk on the spot, by far the largest number of a single talk they had ever sold. The Lord humbles and the Lord exalts according to his good purpose.

After the talk Father Cohen said he was planning the Southern Regional Conference and asked if I would speak in New Orleans. I said I would consider it, and he said that I would hear from him.

Back in Trinidad I was summoned from a meeting by a telephone call from Louisiana. I asked the people with whom I was meeting, "I know I have a serious question to answer. Yes or no? Yes or no? Quickly!"

"Yes," they all said.

On my way to the telephone, I passed the community youth in session and I gave them the same challenge. "I have a serious question coming. Should I answer 'Yes' or 'No'?"

"Yes," they chorused.

It was Father Sam Jacobs, not Father Cohen. He invited me to Lake Charles for their conference Thanksgiving weekend. This was totally unforeseen. But it seemed that since I had already asked for discernment, I had to say yes. Later I also agreed to speak in New Orleans at Father Cohen's conference. God was opening new and unexpected doors.

27

Erica's Wedding...
and Dalmatians

"Mummy," said Erica, phone lines carrying her voice from New York to Trinidad, "Alan and I have set a date for our wedding." Alan was a young Jewish psychologist and teacher, a fine young man.

My head buzzed as I realized that her wedding date was the date of the first Caribbean pastoral institute on the island of Barbados, to which I had already committed.

"Erica, I'm delighted that you and Alan are getting married. But I am afraid that I cannot attend the wedding."

"Oh," she moaned. "But I want you to be there. You *must* be there."

"If you wanted me there," I countered, "you would have discussed your plans with me before making a final decision. As it is, I cannot come. I will do whatever I can for you, but I cannot attend."

"But Mummy, I cannot get married without you."

"Oh, no, all you need is Alan, a priest, and two witnesses. That is what you need. Anything else is superfluous. I am not necessary for your marriage."

She sighed and said softly, "I'll talk to Alan and I'll call you back."

My mother's heart was torn. I really longed to be at that wedding. But I felt that my given word to God and his people could not be broken. He was faithful to me and I wanted to be faithful to him at any price. A few days later Erica rang again to ask if June 29, 1980, would be a convenient date. I assured her that I could arrange it.

Two days before the wedding, my sister Baby and I arrived in New York to meet Alan's parents, who had insisted that they didn't want to meet me as a stranger on the wedding day. Alan's parents, Janice and David, turned out to be gracious hosts, eager to initiate a warm and sincere friendship.

One question burned in my heart, and after dinner I posed it to Janice. "How do you really feel about your son marrying a colored girl?"

"Oh, Babs," she said. She called to her husband, "David, will you come over here, please?" As he joined us, Janice looked at him and said, "David, Babs wants to know how we feel about Alan marrying a colored girl."

He took her hand and replied, "Babs, Alan is a very special son to us. He is a fine young man, and any girl that Alan loves is acceptable to us. To us, Erica is not a colored girl, she is the girl Alan loves. And she must be very special. She is our daughter."

And Janice added, "Please, Babs, never worry about that. Erica is our daughter. You never need to worry."

Erica and Alan had chosen to have a Catholic wedding, to my delight. Alan's family found the arrangement agreeable. Erica asked me to help her to plan the ceremony and to choose the readings. I chose Old Testament readings out of deference to Janice and David. After the wedding Janice said, "Babs, the ceremony was beautiful. I could find nothing objectionable. Thank you."

Alan's parents held the reception at a nice restaurant, and everything was tastefully done. All their family was present; and Titus and Paula and Kemi had flown down from Toronto to join us. During the reception, as the bride and groom visited each table, David gripped my hand and said, eyes shining, "Babs, look at our daughter. Isn't she thoroughly beautiful?" I looked at my own child and discovered a beauty that had newly awakened in her.

A rainstorm raged outside, and I recalled that my mother had said that a tempest raged on the day of her wedding, exactly eighty years prior to this very day. When we celebrated Mama and Papa's fiftieth wedding anniversary it was the same: thunder pealed and lightning flashed and rain poured through the ceiling. Baby and I prayed together that this rain would be a prophetic confirmation that God would bless Erica and Alan with a long life together as he had blessed our parents.

As the happy couple were leaving for their honeymoon, Alan took my hand and said, "Thank you."

"You could never thank me for this in words," I responded. "Your thanks will have to be lived out. The only thanks acceptable would be that you make this marriage work." This was the same fervent hope that I had expressed to Titus when he married Paula.

"I want it to," he said, squeezing my hand.

And it was my turn to say, "Thank you."

Three years later, I kept dreaming about a brood of Dalmatian puppies. I was anxious over one of them. The recurrence of this dream troubled me. I telephoned Alan, thinking I would have some fun with my psychologist son-in-law.

"Alan, in your practice, do you ever work with dreams?"

"Uh huh," he said.

"Can I relate to you a recurrent dream that I've been having?"

"Go ahead."

"I dream about Dalmatian puppies and I worry about one of them."

"Dalmatian puppies would most aptly describe what Erica and I would have if we had children."

"Do you want some Dalmatian puppies?"

"Oh, yes," he said.

"Why didn't you tell me before? I assumed that maybe you and Erica didn't want mixed children. So many educated people make that kind of decision."

"No, no," he said. "We want children."

"Great," I said. "I'll begin to pray."

Two months later, on the last day of the year, Erica called me.

"Mummy," she said, "I am pregnant. I just discovered it and you are the first person I am telling."

"You have been to the doctor?" I asked.

"No, no," she explained. "Alan just did a drugstore test and it's positive."

On August 22, 1984, as we celebrated Paula's thirty-eighth birthday, Chloe Rebecca Bass screamed her way into our world. Erica explained later that she wanted to call her "Ursula," but according to Jewish culture you must not name a baby after a living person, so she named the baby after Alan's deceased paternal grandmother. Having lived this long deprived me of having my name perpetuated; but holding Chloe Rebecca in my arms on her baptismal day filled me with such joy that I gladly relinquished the privilege.

28

The Mystery of Slavery

In 1982 a cry for help came from Ghana through the International Charismatic Renewal Office in Rome. Father Ernst Sievers, a German missionary priest, was seeking people to help him with the charismatic renewal in Ghana. The Rome office felt that Caribbean leaders would better fill this need than Americans because they could bridge the gap between the new world and the old more easily. The request was sent to Father Michael Kosak, still serving on the Caribbean service team in the Virgin Islands. Father Michael immediately called me, remembering that I had had some experience in Africa. Four of us, including Father Kosak, committed to three weeks of concentrated teaching in Ghana.

Immediately after our arrival in Ghana, Father Kosak became ill. I thought he was dying and so did he! The other three of us poured our whole selves into the work of teaching and training and praying over leaders.

One day after I taught on repentance, a big Ashanti man fell on his knees at my feet. He was so tall that when he was kneeling his head was on my breast. Tears streaming down his face, he looked up at me and said, "Mama Babsie, please forgive me for my tribe sending your tribe into exile."

Our tears mingled, but for me they were tears of gratitude to God. "I forgive you with joy," I said to him. At that moment I understood the mystery of slavery—how God could have allowed such an evil. We had left Africa in chains and tears; we came back rejoicing, free persons preaching the liberty of salvation. We brought freedom to those in religious bondage, like the Ashanti man, releasing them from the gods and the customs that enslaved them.

God had used bad black men and bad white men to bring about his own purpose. He brought my ancestors to foreign lands when he could not reach them in their native land. God risked his reputation in dragging them halfway around the world so that he could bring my people to a knowledge of Christ. Our wisdom is foolishness to him. I felt that the incredible gift of Jesus surpassed the atrocious price of slavery.

These days I am praying and asking God to give us his wisdom for today. He must have some answers for the position we find ourselves in.

I embraced the man. Grief and resentment gave way to joy and gratitude.

Discovering Cultural Roots

On the very last day of my stay in Ghana, Father suggested we stop by the post just to check it. We found a letter that had snuck through the unreliable postal system informing me that Paula, Titus, and their children were arriving in Lagos, Nigeria, in a week. When I left for Ghana, I knew Titus planned to return home to Nigeria for a period of service. It had been twenty years since he had left his native land for higher education in Canada. Now his father was growing impatient with Titus's delay, even though he had returned on holiday a few times. His father wrote him, saying, "Son, you went to Canada to become a doctor. Now that you have become a doctor, what do you want to be, God? Why will you not serve your own? When will you come home? Why have you cut yourself away from your own people?" Titus knew that his father's summons could not be ignored. Four things were expected of every good Yoruba man. He was required to bury his father, settle his mother, provide for his siblings, and build a house in his father's village. So he returned and established a hospital. Now he was bringing Paula and the children to live in Africa.

Instead of going home, I went to the airport in Lagos to await Paula's arrival. Because of political unrest the security was tight. I stood in the common area, conscious of being a foreigner and almost afraid to breathe. Suddenly a guard pointed at me.

"You," he commanded, "Come!"

Startled, I said, "Who, me?"

"Yes, you!"

I approached him timidly and asked, "What have I done?"

"You await someone?"

"Yes, my daughter is coming by Swiss Air from Canada."

"Go in," he said, pointing to the restricted area.

My eyes popped out of my head. "In there?"

"Yes," he said pointing again.

I was afraid to go and afraid not to go. I had seen how harshly they dealt with trespassers, but I thought it would be better to obey than to contend. Trembling, I picked my way through the customs area into the immigration area. I saw Paula and Titus approach the immigration officer and my grandchildren playing around. The receiving officer must have asked Paula if this was her first entry into Nigeria. I heard her respond, "Yes, my very first time." Paula looked up and beheld me as she spoke. Her face broke into a smile and she said, "Boys, there's Grandma." Kola and Kunle ran toward me screeching and Kemi followed.

Words cannot express my emotions at that moment. God was blessing me with the joy of an appointment with my loved ones in the midst of serving him. It seemed that the Lord was saying, "I love family. You can trust me to look after your family while you look after mine."

The next two weeks I spent helping Paula settle in and cope with immersion into Nigerian culture. Paula and Titus lived on the third floor of the hospital with temperamental water and electrical service. I played with my grandchildren while Paula met Titus's colleagues and friends. I taught the grandchildren Chinese checkers and within two weeks they were beating me.

According to Nigerian custom, people come to your new home to welcome you. Within a week of Paula's arrival, her mother-in-law visited with a bus load of women all arrayed in their most beautiful native outfits and elegant headdresses. Paula rushed up to my bed, where I was resting.

"Mummy, come, I need you."

I scurried down to find a dozen women in colorful dresses filling the living room, singing to us in their native language and dancing. Meanwhile, Titus's partner's wife, who lived on the second floor, ran down to Titus and said, "Quick, Titus, I think your wife needs you." She sneaked up with a case of soft drinks and biscuits to offer the guests according to the expectation of their culture. Paula had a present for her mother-in-law but was unaware of the custom of giving a gift to all of the visitors. Titus rescued her by quietly arranging with his mother to procure gifts for the visitors.

In the days that followed we met interesting people, rich and poor, including many graduates from England and Canada. Years abroad had had no permanent effect on their concepts of life and living. I attended weddings that were celebrated both in the cultural tradition and in the Church. Through Titus and his family I gained a glimpse of African family life. Even young professionals prostrated themselves before their elders out of deep respect for age and for extended family. Tribal loyalties were almost as strong as filial bonds. God blessed me with deep insights into my own ethnic roots, and it became easier to understand some Caribbean attitudes. Neither time nor distance had been able to separate completely us from our roots.

29

A Drop's Quest to Rejoin the Ocean

I sat on a promontory of rock jutting out into the sea. On one side the sea raged, banging into rocks, lashing against the shore. The water there, where the Atlantic Ocean and Caribbean Sea meet, is treacherous all the time. On the other side of the rock the water is shimmering, peaceful.

As I looked at the sea, the Lord said to me, "Babsie, you are a drop of water that became detached from the ocean, but the sound of the ocean remained in your ear. Your whole life has been a quest to rejoin the ocean."

I gazed upon the anger of the ocean's waves. Knowing my own natural tendency to anger, I asked, "Lord, is it only the anger of the sea that I have, is my anger the only characteristic of the sea that I have retained?"

"No, no. All the characteristics of the ocean are in the drop."

I began to weep, recalling the number of times I had been angry like the ocean, like a tiger wanting to break its bonds. I recalled the times my response to life had been like the ocean dashing itself against the rock. I wept hot tears. But the Lord continued.

"A drop of water in the ocean knows itself, and the nature of the ocean is in the drop. Wherever the ocean is blessed, the drop is blessed. Wherever the ocean is cursed, the drop is cursed. Your life has been a quest to rejoin the ocean. And all your relationships have been formed in the hope that they would reunite you to the ocean.

"From age to age I reserve a people who would bless me. Wherever I am blessed, you are blessed, because you are in me. Your journey has been your quest to rejoin the ocean."

Then I saw myself as a little drop running to every puddle and asking, "Are you the ocean? Are *you* the ocean?" I had spent my life running around looking for love and friendship and identity in things that weren't big enough to satisfy me. Every time I thought I had found the ocean and plunged into it, I discovered that it was only a puddle. Lio was too small. Tommy was too small. A puddle by itself could not satisfy. Only the ocean. Only God.

The Tiger Within

God cancels all our sins. He also takes our weaknesses and shows forth his glory through them as he works with us to transform them into virtues.

God created Adam by himself. He could have created

Eve the same way. But no, God has tied himself to us his children in such a manner that he is committed not to do anything without our help and cooperation. He can do it by himself, but he chooses to tie himself to us, to seek our cooperation and good will. God made Eve, so to speak, with the help of Adam. Because Adam had been made in the image and likeness of God, when Adam saw Eve he said: "I like! Very good! Very good!"

God calls us where we are, but he loves us too much to leave us there. He loves us and fills us with his gifts; but he desires to transform us. As his sons and daughters we should yearn to show forth the characteristics of his family made manifest in Jesus and reflected so brightly in Mary.

Early in my childhood, anger manifested itself in a powerful way. I excused myself on the grounds that I had inherited rage from my father, and I almost boasted that I had a familial right to it. I argued that my wrath was almost always righteous, a reaction to injustice of some kind. But after the incident with my brother Henry, I tried hard to restrain my fury and smiled through many an awkward situation.

Once one of my friends at work asked why I never got vexed. She tried to convince me that my nonchalant attitude could easily make me a doormat. I laughed and explained that when I was exasperated I wasn't pretty. I prayed that she would never see me irritated. She didn't take me at all seriously until one day she saw an outburst that made everybody in the office remain as quiet as mice for the rest of the day. I had

had a flash of rage against my boss. I broke the restraint that I had exercised. That evening when she was leaving for home she whispered in my ear, "Never get angry again, never."

My fury raged like a tiger in a tank. As long as I could keep the lid on, it remained asleep. But once in a while it would break the leash and escape. With the new life in the Holy Spirit I was living, I really hoped that I had seen the last of it. But every day I discovered that community is the best factory for transforming sinners into saints. It is a place of whittling and chiselling and continual dying to self.

One day a community member had an appointment with an Irish priest to visit the sick. I realized from her schedule that it would be impossible for her to keep this commitment. I drew it to her attention and asked her to change the time. A few days later I checked and she hadn't done it. I pointed out that this priest was a stickler for time and that the community would be put in a bad light should she fail to honor her commitment. Having talked to her about it three times, I assumed she had taken responsible action.

On the morning of the appointment, I was preparing to go to the city on community business. I was standing in the kitchen drinking coffee when I heard a car pull up and the toot of a horn. A few moments later I heard a car door slam and the car take off in such a manner that I knew that whoever was in the car was in a rage. I just knew that it was the priest who had come at the appointed time and left in anger, just as I had foretold it.

When a community member came into the kitchen to announce that this very thing had happened, I flew into a rage. I threw the cup across the room. Coffee splashed everywhere and the cup shattered into a million pieces.

"I knew this was going to happen. I knew this would happen. If I saw her now, I would kill her with my own two hands! She has no respect at all. She doesn't care what the Church thinks about this community. I would run the car straight over her, if I could see her now!"

I tore out of the house into my car and rammed it into gear. The car took off with a leap and a jump. I drove all the way to the city steaming in fury. When I neared my destination, I realized that I would need to park on the main street, and I had never procured a parking place without praying. I began to talk to God.

"Lord," I said, "normally on coming to the city I pray for a parking space, and you have never failed me. But my behavior today has been so reprehensible that I have no merits on which I could come before your throne. Nevertheless, on the merits of Jesus, your Son, I dare to plead for a parking space," I queried. "If you can see your way to give it to me, I will thank you. But if not, it's okay, I will understand."

In a few minutes, I arrived at the building at which I needed to stop. To my shock I saw red parking lights go on in the back of a big car, twice the size of my own. He glided out and I pulled right in. I couldn't believe it. I was smack in front of the main door of the building. As I bent over to take the key from the ignition, the person I needed to see walked out of the door and said, "Auntie Babsie, what are you doing here?"

"Why are you out here?"

"I don't know," she said. "I just felt I should walk out here, and here you are."

God had not only brought me to a perfect parking place, but he brought out to me the very person I needed to see—in spite of my despicable condition. What kind of God is this that could give the best to such a great sinner in the midst of her sin?

I completed my business right in the car, then drove off. I wept all the way back home.

At home I asked the woman at whom I had been so angry to meet me in the prayer room. As soon as I began to talk, she interrupted with vain excuses. I knew she was lying. As she continued to hold her point defiantly, refusing to admit her misdemeanor and repent, I felt the tiger come alive again. I glared at her.

"Look, look, this beast is coming alive in me again! Run. Run or I'll kill you!"

She ran in terror. I knew that I needed the power of God to get rid of this demon.

"Lord, can you see the headlines tomorrow if I kill someone? Can you imagine the archbishop's plight and shame if this uncontrollable anger wins out? I need your help. Please help me. Kill this beast inside. I cannot afford to let this ire continue to rage inside of me." I wept bitterly.

Suddenly his presence filled the room. Gently he said, "Pray for compassion. You lack compassion. When someone acts foolishly, your response is 'Get rid of them. They are useless,' instead of 'What a pity, that's all they can do.' Pray for compassion and it will be given to you."

Since then I continually pray for the gift of compassion, and I have found it increasingly easy to overlook the weaknesses of others. Through the years I have not had another such bout of anger; and this sister still lives and breathes. Praise Jesus!

A Critical Spirit

The Lord exhorts us to enter his presence with thanksgiving in our hearts. I had to pray for an attitude of thanksgiving. By nature I have a critical spirit, a spirit that could find fault with everything. No matter what people did, or what God did, I could come in and find what wasn't done. "You give marvelous comrades to me," we sing. I used to say, "Lord, where are these comrades you have promised? I am surrounded by drips." And my spirit can easily find fault with what I am and am not.

God encourages us to delight in what we have and not to complain about what we haven't. I had to pray for the grace of gratitude, and thank God, he has released gratitude in me and caused it to flow. We need to be grateful for God revealing himself to us and revealing ourselves to us and showing us our need of him. And as we come to know God, we begin to magnify him for who he is, not just what he gives.

When I was a child, I used to wish I were Shirley

Temple. I liked her curls, I liked all the things she did, and most of all I liked the approval that she got from the crowds. But I had to give it up because I didn't have her curls, I didn't have her complexion, I didn't have anything that she had. One night several years ago, just before speaking to five hundred or so priests and deacons in Steubenville, Ohio, I recalled this childhood desire of mine, and I felt God telling me, "All the time I had reserved a place for you that no one can take away."

I don't have to wish I were anybody else, but desire that God will bring me what he meant for me from the beginning, what he had in his mind for me when he first conceived of me. I pray that I might, day by day, allow God to bring forth in me all the hidden treasures that were there before my parents set eyes on me. He saw me, knew me, invested in me, and was excited about showing me forth on the day of my birth.

God's Bulldozer

Through my whole life I have had the dubious privilege of initiating new things and renewing the old. And always, once things are on track, it seems there are countless hands ready to push me away. My mother used to comment that I was always opening ways for others to run in while I was being left behind. I observed this phenomenon over and over again in my life, but I didn't know what I could do about it and I wasn't even sure that I should do anything about it. I couldn't help wishing that my efforts would come to an end more pleasantly.

In one such experience, I befriended a young woman who was going through a messy, painful divorce. I placed all my resources at her disposal to make the way easier for her. I invested long hours counseling and comforting her to the extent that one night after leaving her I fell asleep at the wheel. Only God's mercy protected me from a fatal automobile accident.

As soon as she was out of the woods, she began to show in unmistakable ways that I was no longer necessary to her. I tried to understand what was happening to our friendship, to no avail.

One day I suggested, "Let's take a week apart from one another. I will not call you at all. You can call me if you need me and I will be there for you. Let us use the time to pray, asking God to show us where this friction is coming from."

At the end of the week when we got together she blurted, "Babs, you are a bulldozer!"

Cut to the quick, I asked, "Is that how you experience me?"

"Yes."

"A bulldozer?" I repeated. "But that is the last thing I want to be."

"I am sorry, Babs." Before she could proceed further, I said, "No, no, don't be sorry. I will go to God with it. And if he says what you say, I will be the first to repent. He knows that that's the last thing I want to be."

I felt like a bird that had fallen into a pool of icy cold,

deep water, hardly able to lift its wings from the weight of them. That night in the prayer room I pleaded with God.

"Lord, did you hear what she said?" I rehearsed in his ear all that had happened. "She called me a bulldozer! That's the last thing I want to be." (I'm sure I heard the Lord chuckle as I listened for him.)

"The kingdom of God needs bulldozers, too. What city can be built without a bulldozer?"

He opened my spiritual eyes. I saw an empty lot filled with wild grass. A bulldozer was parked there, its teeth filled with mud. It was a picture of dejection. On the adjoining lot there was a big building, maybe a cathedral, being built, soaring to the heavens. I knew then that my call was to be a pioneer. Once the foundation was laid I was to get out of the way and not wait for people to ask me to move off. Tears of disappointment flowed from my eyes, but my heart began a shout of exultant joy. To know the truth is to be set free.

In that moment I could look back and laugh at all the instances in which I had suffered rebuff and walked away dejected from works I had initiated. I knew that I would never again go through that kind of suffering. Knowing when to move out of the way is a priceless gift, and I was beginning to lay hold of it. Mine was the call to give joyfully and to leave joyfully, asking for nothing in return.

Several years later, a priest said to me, "Babs, what's wrong with the renewal is wrong with you!"

Because of my bulldozer vision, I was free to respond to him, "Father, thank you for speaking to me so freely. I will take it to the Lord. And if what you say is true, I will have no trouble disappearing from the scene."

That time I found that he had spoken out of his own emotion, and I was free to continue on in the work at hand. God apparently had more earth to move in this situation. His bulldozer had not been dismissed.

Blotting out Sin

There have been times when I've sinned, been remorseful, and gone to confession—but I was sorry only insofar as I'd been found out. Those times I was sorry because it made me think less of myself.

My little grandson made his first confession at age seven. Beforehand I asked him, "Are you afraid?"

"Yes," he said.

"Is it because you don't know your sins?"

"No, Grams," he said, "I know all my sins and I know my brother's sins too."

"Then why are you afraid? Father will be like Jesus to you. Father will be full of compassion. Just go to him, tell him your sins, he will pray with you, and everything will be okay. Jesus will forgive you your sins."

An hour after he returned from his first confession, I asked him, "How was it?"

He said, "Good."

"Was Father like Jesus to you?"

"Yes."

"How do you feel?"

He looked at me steadily; and then he jumped into the air and shouted, "Gram, I have no sin! No sin! My sins are washed away, Grams. I have no sin!"

As I hugged him and congratulated him, I wondered if this child understood. One morning a week later, like a typical little boy, he decided he wanted cake before eating breakfast. I told him, "You can't. You have to wait."

He sulked, "I want it now. I'm never going to eat any breakfast. Unless I get the cake, I won't eat any breakfast."

So I said to him, "Your sins were washed away last week, and now you are surely putting stains back on your soul. Jesus is standing by, looking at you, and he doesn't like this at all. And if you continue, you'll have to go right back to confession."

My grandson immediately became remorseful. "I'm sorry Grams." He understood what sin does.

I next saw my grandson when he was eleven years old. During my stay he was heading off to church to go to confession. I told him, "I'm so glad to see you going to confession so easily."

He responded, "I always go," and left.

Upon his return, he sat on my lap, looked up at me, and asked, "Grams, isn't it true that you can't really be sorry for sin until you understand how you've hurt God?"

Repentance is a gift of God. It comes when you understand how you hurt God and disrupt the Body of Christ.

One time God was dealing with me on repentance. He showed me through the Scriptures that the only way to wash away sin was with the precious Blood of Jesus Christ. Then God said to me, "Do you think if I gave you a bowl of blood with a sponge, you could retrace your steps, go right back through your life, and blot out all the marks that you have made in the lives of other people?"

I said, "I could try." I tried to do this in the Spirit, thinking of all the people that my disobedience had wounded. I thought I was finished, and I cried out victoriously, "It's over!"

He said, "No, let's go to Africa."

"But Lord, I've never been there. I don't know anybody there." (This was before my missions.)

"Yes, you do."

"Who?" Then, in the Spirit, I was reminded of a girl (now a nun) who grew up with my children, and whose faith was shaken when I was divorced. The fact that I had not sought divorce was immaterial to this child. The simple fact of it shook her faith.

The Lord continued: "Now she's a teacher in Africa. The wound you inflicted upon her faith is affecting all the children that's she teaching." I began to cry. He said, "Don't cry. Don't cry, because now that you have come to understand the effects of sin and what a long tail sin has, and how it could affect generations yet unborn, how your sin could mark and affect the lives of others—now," he said, "that you have understood the wound your sin makes in the Body of Christ, I will help you. Now that you have shed tears of repentance, through forgiveness I will blot out the effects of your sin."

Through this experience with God, I came to realize that there is no sin so scarlet that God cannot forgive and blot out completely if we have the gift of repentance.

Overcoming Demons

In Trinidad we have two exorcists who have been appointed by the bishop. When we have trouble with someone to whom we are ministering, we go to the exorcists to pray and gain their assistance in discerning whether the devil is at work. One woman had been prayed with for some time for deliverance. Finally someone took her to a psychiatrist, who put her on a diet including certain vitamins, and she was completely healed.

We shouldn't jump to conclusions that bad things are always caused by evil spirits. We should look for natural causes. Some of us feel that if we have a headache, it's the devil. If you stub your toe, it's the devil. Well, if you belong to God, how come the devil has so much power over you? I don't look for demons, I look for Jesus.

30

Praying Always

When God first called me to this new life in the Spirit, he said to me through Father Duffy, "Pray always." Saint Paul, too, says, "Pray always." My response was, "Well, you can't pray all the time. Paul didn't mean that." But the more I allow myself to be led by the Holy Spirit, the more I realize that you *can* pray all the time, especially since we've been given the gift of tongues. Now I continually pray to the Holy Spirit. I pray my favorite prayer all day long, trying to keep an attitude of prayer.

I was at a funeral in a Protestant church and they sang a song with the words, "Teach me to pray, Lord. Teach me to pray." After the funeral I asked the choirmaster, "Could you please give me a copy of that hymn?" And I asked him to sing it once again, and he did. I made that song my prayer for a long time. Every time I experience dryness in prayer, I pray it:

Teach me to pray, Lord. Teach me to pray.
This is my heart's cry day unto day.
I long to know Thy will and Thy way.
Teach me to pray, Lord. Teach me to pray.

Power in prayer, Lord. Power in prayer
Here, mid earth's sin and sorrow and cares
Men lost and dying, souls in despair.
O grant me Thy power, power in prayer.

I must confess that in nearly thirty years of really trying to follow the direction of the Holy Spirit in prayer, I
have not come to a place where I can pray every day at
the same hour, except for Mass. Although I know that
this is an extremely worthwhile aim, no matter what time
I wake up, even if I promise myself that I will pray at four
o'clock in the morning, I can be sure that at ten past four
the phone will ring. If I tell myself I'm going to pray at
midnight, I can be sure there is a distraction—the dogs
begin to bark, there is an intruder, somebody needs help.
And so I have never been able to pray at the same time
each day, yet God has given me the grace of a good
prayer life.

As regards distractions, I have found that many a
time what seems like a distraction can be an urge of
the Holy Spirit to pray about something or for something. I once read an article by a priest who advised
that we try to incorporate our distractions in our
prayer. I was praying one day when something I had not
thought about for a long time entered my mind and I
couldn't get it out. I decided to try Father's advice and

incorporate it in my prayer. The next day it all came to pass, and I knew that God had wanted me to pray about it because it was coming up. A thought comes up, and soon afterwards God enfleshes that thought—the person I thought about turns up, or I receive a letter. Before I knew God, I suppose it's what I would have called telepathy.

Make My Word Your Home

God said to me one night while I was in prayer, "Make my Word your home."

Now, the Word of God for me is the most beautiful gift that I have been given. But I said, "That's a hard word."

And he said, "Yes. Suppose you got home one night and the house was locked and you had no key to get in, would you say, 'This is a hard deal, maybe I don't live here,' and proceed to walk all around the town looking for your house?"

And I said, "I wouldn't do that," because I recalled a night that I had come home keyless to a locked house. I tried every door and every window, to no avail, so I began to pray. I was inspired to go to my sister's house— which had about a hundred doors. I took every key she had, went back home, and tried each key until one fit.

Then God said, "That is the same way you must feel about my Word. Be determined to enter it and then let it abide in your heart. Let it find a home in your heart. Ask me for the key. I will give it to you."

Journey through Darkness

There are times when I wonder if I had been dreaming when all the exhilaration of the Spirit filled me, when life took on a glorious turn, when the sunsets were more beautiful and the sunrises brighter. I saw so many beautiful things when my eyes were opened to the spiritual life. But later life became dull, and I actually began to question myself: Was all this for real? A kind of a darkness fell over me.

I stopped at the church one morning and said to God, "I cannot continue like this. I have tasted of your sweetness. I have walked in the light for all this time. Now the darkness is completely unacceptable. You've got to help me." As I sat there crying out from the depths of my spirit, "Help! Help!" I decided to open the Scriptures. I opened to Psalm 63, in which David cried out to the Lord, "My soul longs for you like dry land for water." I realized that if David, "a man after God's own heart," came to a place of such longing, that it was okay for me to long for God. I realized that the God that I knew when I first gave my life to Jesus was no longer sufficient. My heart was longing for something more complete—for a deeper knowledge of God, a deeper relationship with him.

Jesus said, "Blessed are they who hunger and thirst for righteousness for they shall have their fill." God says: "If you seek me, you shall find me when you have sought me with all your heart." I realized in that moment that it was a time of more intense seeking for me, a time of digging deeper in a well that had seemingly run dry.

God's grace had not run out, only the feeling of God's presence with me each moment had ceased. My prayer changed. I began praying the prayer of David and saying to God, "See, I am seeking you with all my heart. I seek you alone. Nothing else will satisfy me." Indeed, once I had touched the wells of living water, touched the sea of the love of God, no other love would satisfy me, no created thing could fill the longing in my heart for God.

God is infinite. The more we discover him, the more we must discover him. But we can't make new discoveries unless he allows us to tire of that which we have already received. Then our souls begin to long again and he satisfies our thirst by revealing himself to us in a more captivating way. God desires with all his heart that man should come to know him fully, that we should love him and live in his presence in great joy.

My prayer changed and God returned. When he returned to me in a conscious way, I saw him more glorious, more loving, more powerful, more wonderful than I had seen him before. The dark night of my soul was God inviting me to come up higher: "Come up higher—there is more!" When a child is standing on the ground looking above, and the branches of the trees prevent him from seeing the beauty of the sky, if he climbs the tree, the higher he goes the more beauty of the sky does he see.

Another time I felt I was in darkness, yet there was evidence of God's presence all the time. Always there was a sign that he was nearby, but his intimate, personal presence in my life seemed to have receded. I went into my prayer room and began to cry out to him: "Where are you? I am longing for you! It is dark all around me. I want to see you again. I cannot live in darkness."

And the presence of the Lord came down upon me, and the Lord said to me: "You are the light of the world. The light doesn't see. The light shines that others may see. Shine on."

And I said, "Okay. I'll be content with that. I'll keep on shining. I'll keep on smiling even though I don't feel like smiling. I'll keep on professing my faith in you even though I don't see you because faith is not sight."

We must desire to come through the darkness. We must remember what it was like when God first came into our lives. We know that this God is the same yesterday, today, and forever. We recall what we had. We affirm that we are grateful for his living, loving presence that was so real to us. "Lord, I am so grateful that I have experienced you. Now I am missing you and I want you back. You promised that you would never leave me. Lord, I need you. I want you. I do not want to live without you." When God sees that this is the desire of our hearts, God returns and shows himself to us more deeply.

Friendship with God is a deep relationship. God wants to have us as friends. He wants to be able to ask us for help, to be able to tell us what his own longings are. When you have an intimate friend, you can share your life with him, unafraid of betrayal. Just so, I have learned, does God want to make a friend out of me. In this way I can participate in his life to the fullest, and he can ask me to help him bring other souls to Christ. God desires to reveal himself to me, to you, completely.

How? At what cost? Our hearts. We have to seek intimacy with him ourselves because he will not force himself on us.

I have found that each time of dryness is a time to learn how dull life can become without Christ. It motivates me into deeper and purer prayer. Our prayer as children is, "Gimme, gimme, gimme." Our prayer is not mature until we can ask God, "What do you want? What can I do for you? I have come to do your will." This stems from confidence that the will of God is the safest place for us to be.

The Slaughter of the Innocents

One day in 1990 I was praying my daily prayers in the prayer room. For a while I had been having a sense of ennui, futility. I said to the Lord, "Reveal to me a new truth or highlight some old truth that would give me some stimulation. Make me excited about life in the Spirit again." I waited and waited, praying to the Holy Spirit, but nothing happened.

So finally I said, "Okay, give me a word that would sustain me today." I reached for the Bible, and it fell upon the slaughter of the innocents (Mt 2:16–18). After reading it I asked, "What bearing could this have on anything today, what do you want to say about it?"

I experienced a nudge, like someone touched me on the elbow: "Do you know any other time innocents were slaughtered?"

"Yes, at the birth of Moses."

"Whose children were slaughtered?"

"The children of the chosen people."

Again he nudged. "And when again?"

I said, "The night of the Passover. The slaughter of the first born. Surely some of those children were innocent."

He said, "Whose children were slaughtered?"

"The children of the Egyptians, the children of the unrighteous."

"And what happened then?"

I said, "There was a passover for the people of God, there was a passover from the land of Egypt to the land of Canaan, from slavery into freedom."

Then he said, "What happened in the time of Moses?"

"The enemy saw that the deliverer was coming and tried to frustrate the plan of God by killing the children of the Hebrews."

"But what happened then?"

"Moses was saved, and the people of God passed over."

He said, "And what happened at the time of Herod?"

"Jesus was saved, the Deliverer was saved again, and the people of God passed over from Judaism into Christianity."

"Babsie, look around you."

"O my God! The innocents are being slaughtered on every side, the children of the righteous and the unrighteous."

And he said, "Babsie, Israel is passing over."

I knew that he meant from a Church of weakness to a Church of power. The sons of God are about to be revealed. Creation is groaning, but it will come to pass.

"Creation waits with eager longing for the revealing of the sons of God" (Rm 8:19 RSVCE).

He said, "I can deal with the innocents, but pray for the Herods. Prayer for the Herods brings about conversions."

31

Expanding the Family

I had always dreamed of having a large family, and I had prayed many long prayers to have a son. God sent two beautiful daughters eleven months apart, and that was all. It seemed that God had forgotten the rest of my prayer. But in this new life in the Holy Spirit he sent me many sons and daughters. I expanded the tent pegs of my heart again and again. The stakes lengthened to accommodate the people God would send my way who needed a spiritual mother.

After a Life in the Spirit Seminar, an eighty-four-year-old toothless man looked at me and said, "Mother."

"How could I ever be a mother to him?" I thought.

As if reading my mind, he said, "You are my mother, you know. You did more than my own mother ever did. You brought me to Jesus." And tears streamed quietly down his face. In that instant I grasped the meaning of the mystery of motherhood and the role of Mary in the family of God. In this miracle of new birth there was no barrier of age or race, culture or social status, economics or education. In Christ all are one. And those who bring others to Christ are mothers and fathers in the kingdom of God.

Brothers and sisters from around the world have visited our house and our community, including priests, bishops, sisters and lay people. Many of them have called me "Mama." Every man, woman, or child that has been blessed in our apostolate has become flesh and blood to me, so that my family has no bounds.

I was invited to the chaplaincy of the University of the West Indies to speak to the students about the charismatic renewal. Soon after meeting this college group, I became spiritual director for two of the young men; they are both now priests. In trying to foster life, it is inevitable that we should pray for and advocate vocations. Everywhere that God has led me, I have encouraged young men and women to pray and seek the Lord to follow their vocations courageously. I assure them that God who calls them is faithful and will be sure to bring to completion the good work he has begun in them.

During a round table discussion on women and the priesthood, someone said to me, "I don't think you will live long enough to see women priests ordained."

"I have no aspiration to be a priest," I retorted. "I am the mother of priests and that is privilege enough for me."

I was asked to speak to the priests in Rome at the International Priests' Retreat in 1990. I was told that the Vatican would have to approve me as a woman speaker. So I said yes; since Mother Teresa had been the only woman up to that time who had been allowed to address the priests, I could not imagine that approval would ever be given for me.

Some months later I received a formal invitation to speak. I felt the terror of a nightmare. What could I say to these men? I couldn't teach them. They were *my* teachers. I couldn't preach to them. They were my fathers. But I knew that God wanted to say something. I tried to wrest from the heart of God a message that would be meaningful to them.

God did not fail me. I addressed the priests as my fathers, my brothers, my friends, my sons. "Had I known nineteen years ago when I gave my life to God that great moments like this would come, I think I might have hesitated out of fear! Thanks be to God who hides up his sleeves the things that he will do and woos us with a tenderness and a love like we have never known before."

I called them fathers because they brought me to life in Baptism, nurtured that life with the Eucharist, and instructed me with the word of God. I called them brothers because we are members of the same family of God, the Church, sons and daughters of the Father and children of Mary. I called them friends because in confession, when they have seen me as I am, they did not reject me but offered the Lord's forgiveness. And I called them sons because, "by a miracle of grace, each one of you has become a son to me. I feel that I've given birth to each of you through a miracle of God's grace."

I spoke to them of Columbus's discovery of Trinidad and of the missionaries from Spain, France, and Ireland

that brought the faith to our island. I told them of the
work God was doing in the Caribbean even now. "He is
teaching those who were slaves how to become masters
in the kingdom of God by reminding us that Jesus took
on our deepest cares and hurts. The Prince of Peace, the
God of heaven and earth, the Lord from whom all things
were made and in whom all things have been created,
became a slave so that he might teach us step by step how
to shake off the shame and the degradation of every kind
of slavery."

I addressed the thought that they were deprived of children. "As fathers of the Church you have brought forth
thousands of children unto God. My brothers, my sons,
my beautiful fathers, God loves you with an intense love.
There is no joy more supreme than to be called and chosen by the Most High God. Every time you bring a soul to
Christ, every time you pour water from the baptismal
fountain, heaven looks on with supreme joy and the Lord
is pleased."

I had tried to make the Church my hiding place, my
place of rest. "It was only when I found Jesus that I knew
what real rest was. God is saying that your burden, your
work, is to make Christ known, and that if you cease to
do this you are useless. He is commissioning you again
now, asking you to gaze upon Christ and be transformed
by the light that comes from his visitation. Spend your
time in his presence, weep before him, and let him cleanse
you in his precious Blood. Your greatness is your faith.
Our greatness as Christians is always our faith and our
love."

I consider that talk the crowning experience in my life. It was as if God had prepared me for that moment with every aspect of my life: my Caribbean culture, the color of my skin, my experience of the Church before Vatican II, my work in the charismatic renewal, my spiritual motherhood—all that I might pass on God's enduring love to these his laborers in his vineyard, that I might encourage them in their "yes" to his plan.

Make Yahweh Your Only Joy

There's a young charismatic priest in our house, Father Michael Moses, who was ordained in 1988. After his ordination he asked the bishop to let him live with us, and the bishop agreed. Father Mike had told me he was going to request this, and I had simply said, "You'll never get that."

He retorted with, "Well, Auntie Babsie, Psalm 37:4 says, 'Make Yahweh your only joy and he will give you the desires of your heart.' And God knows that he's my only joy. And God knows the desire of my heart is to live with you so that you can continue to direct me."

Father Mike was my delight. I had never seen anyone so happy as was this priest the first two months of his ordained life. To see this young man embrace the priesthood with such joy, to see him baptize a baby—when he poured the water on the baby, it was as if he would drown the poor infant, so much water did he use. So I said to him, "You doused that baby good."

And he said, "Yes. I had a singular thrill as I was pouring the water on that child. I felt as if I was giving birth to the child, as if I myself had fathered that child. I just wanted to give the baby to God!"

"Ah," I said to myself, "that's the secret of being a father." He went from one baptism to the next with joy.

One day he came back from Mass and said, "Incredible! Incredible to think that in my hands bread and wine become the Body and Blood of Jesus Christ. I cannot believe it!" He was skipping like a ram.

I thought, "The mystery, the incredible mystery."

The first time he heard confessions, he said, "To think, Babsie, that I can give absolution to someone and through me God absolves sin." The beauty of the priesthood was so fresh and sweet.

Two months later, he crashed. A depression hit him that was wild, unreasonable. He could not be consoled, day or night. He would perk up just to celebrate Mass, and right after Mass he would again plummet to the depths of depression. He had an uncle who was mentally ill, so the first thing that came to him was that maybe mental illness runs in his family and he too is becoming mentally ill.

He would ask me, "Do you think I am going mad?"

I would answer, "I don't know. I am afraid."

"No! No, it can't be. I will not go mad. I can't go mad."

"You hold the key right there in your hands. The psychologists say that if you say no to madness, you can never go mad. And you say no." There's a freedom in the theory that I like.

Every time he had to preach or teach, the power of God would come upon him and he would do an excellent job. Each time he finished, he zoomed down into depression. He suffered this way for about five months.

One day as I was praying for him, I asked God for an answer. God said, "I shall not suffer my holy one to see corruption." There was no outward sign at all that this could be true, but I told Father Michael and he held on to that word.

Every time his spirit was oppressed, he would come to me with tears in his eyes and ask me, "Did God really tell you 'I will not suffer my holy one to see corruption'?"

And I would say, "Yes, God told me that."

Finally, God said to me, "I gave him to you like I gave John to Mary."

And I said to God, "How could this be?" And I began to ask God to reveal to me the mystery of the giving of John to Mary. For the first time it occurred to me what condition John must have been in when the Master died on the cross before John's eyes. This young boy had placed all his hope in Jesus and whatever he promised. And suddenly it was over. It was finished. There was nothing. His feeling of dejection must have been unfathomable. So Jesus gave him to Mary. What must Mary have gone through? In the face of her own grief, she now had a broken man on her hands. She became his mother. She held him over those three days while Jesus was in the tomb. She had to forget about herself. I understood then that it was okay for me to hold this young priest when he cried and to let him cry until the hour of his deliverance came. I had been afraid to do so.

The time passed. The darkness lifted. God delivered him. He came through this trial with shining colors. And he said to me, "I was amazed to know all the gunk that was inside of me. I never thought that inside of me there was an inferno like that. I used to think I was a pretty good man. And I thought I was a great priest until God brought me through the iron furnace."

Today this young priest is full of compassion. He said to me recently, "I know that what God was teaching me was the grace of compassion. He has taken from me all my critical nature and brought me to the place where I have compassion for others who are weak and others who are hurting." That was the only way that God could do it, and he did.

Father Michael has become my father, my son, my brother, and my friend, as well as father to the whole community. He is much loved by the old and the young. Little children warm up to him easily. He works assiduously with a group of young men, called "The Young Christophers," trying to give them goals and purpose for creative and healthy living. Though few in number, because many young people shirk the discipline that he requires in dress and conduct, nevertheless they have been of great service to the Church and the community. Five of them received scholarships from Franciscan University of Steubenville to attend the Pope's World Youth Day in Denver in 1993. They played their steel pans for Cardinal Bernard Law and at many private Masses. It was a great experience for them. They play football and write a newsletter. Father Mike hopes that out of this bunch of young men will come fathers of strong families and vocations to the priesthood.

He also works with teenage girls in the community, trying to foster trust and friendship. These young women are called "The Fleurettes," or the little flowers of Saint Theresa.

Father Michael arrived in community when I needed a strong and reliable friend and through him, God has met that need. In both my marriages I was looking for friendship above all. Friendship will get you through. Father Michael and I have had differences. But he doesn't let the sun go down on his wrath. He has taught me what it is to have a good marriage—he has taught me more about marriage than two marriages did.

He Will Grant You Your Heart's Desire

Trinidad was undergoing a recession in the 1980s. Five of our dollars were worth just one U. S. dollar. There were many things we didn't get because of this. One day Father Michael said, "Gee. I am longing for a Mars." He loves Mars candy bars. I said nothing. Two days later: "Gee. I'm longing for a Mars Bar. Auntie Babsie, we really have no Mars Bars?" A couple of hours later, "Lord, I said I want a Mars Bar."

So I said, "Michael, there are no Mars in Trinidad. Get it straight. No Mars in Trinidad."

He said, "Excuse me, I'm not talking to you, I'm talking to God."

The following day people sent for Father Michael to pray with a man who was very ill. The people there tried to give him some things to honor him (we love our priests and we are always bringing them little gifts); but he said, "No, no, I just want to pray with this man and minister to him."

But before he left, they gave him a little plastic bag. He brought it home and said to me, "Look in that bag. I think I see Snickers there. I think I see Snickers through the plastic." And indeed, when I opened the bag, I found Snickers in it. So Father Michael said, "Gee. This is incredible. I ask for Mars and I get Snickers."

So I said, "Well, I prefer Snickers anyhow."

"I suppose God is giving me Snickers so you can have what you like best."

"Isn't that good enough for you?"

"Yes, I suppose for your sake I'll have to take the Snickers." Then he said, "Lord, I really asked for Mars."

We didn't eat the Snickers bars. For some reason we just put down the bag. The following night friends came from America to visit us. As soon as one of the women began to unpack, she said, "Where is the candy?" She rummaged through a bag and pulled out a Mars Bar.

Father Michael announced triumphantly, "I told you! Make Yahweh your only joy and he will give you the desires of your heart!"

Father Michael comes from a well-to-do family, but our community is poor. As I've mentioned, there's a special, thick soup we make for Sunday dinner, callaloo. For callaloo to be perfect, it must have crab meat in it. But crabs have become so expensive that years ago I stopped buying crabs; but I make the dish every Sunday anyway.

One day Father Michael inquired of me, "Auntie Babsie, how is it that when I was at my mother's house, I got crab in my callaloo every Sunday, but since I've been here, I've been getting callaloo but no crab?"

"Well, your family is rich. You can go back there and eat every Sunday, but I cannot afford crab."

He responded, "I live here; I am not going back. I have taken a vow of poverty. But I know callaloo has to have crab in it. God knows he's my only joy and he's going to provide crab for me right here in this house."

I laughed and said, "Let's see."

Two weeks later, we headed up into the mountains to pay someone a visit. As our four-wheel-drive vehicle climbed the steep and narrow road, the first rain of the season came. Crabs began running all over the mountainside. So I said to the young priest, "Father, there's crabs. Catch them."

He looked at me and said, "But I don't know *how* to catch crabs."

The driver overheard us and piped up, "Reverend, you want crabs?"

"Yes," Father replied.

"Come over here, I'll teach you how to catch them."

The driver stopped, the two of them got out, and in no time at all the truck was full of crabs. When we got home, we had crabs in the callaloo, curried crabs, all kinds of crab dishes. Every time the young priest ate crab, he said to me, "I told you that if you make Yahweh your only joy, he will grant you your heart's desire."

32

Miracles and Healing

As I continued to strive to respond to the call of God and to live the radical gospel, I discovered that it was quite impossible to do so without coming to grips with the needs and the pain of all people. The hungry needed bread, the naked clothing, the ignorant instruction, and the homeless shelter. Daily I grew in awareness of the corporal needs of those all around me. Many things could be accomplished by prayer alone, but many others demanded prayer and hands on hard work and death to self.

It was common for people to request prayer for physical healing and I saw God work many healing miracles. My approach has become simple: I pray for all I'm worth and leave the healing up to Jesus. I do not have to apologize for his action, nor reproach anyone for lack of faith. God has healed so many times when my own faith was inadequate that I know the faith of Jesus is sufficient for any healing in the will of God to be effected.

I am never really anxious to pray for healing. For me the biggest healing is in the souls and hearts of men. My anxiety is that people should come to the knowledge of Christ and his personal love for them. My soul yearns to capture hearts for God and to see men and women rise up to praise him and glorify him. I long to see us make the Body of Christ both visible and effective among the poor and the rich alike.

I have seen the dead raised to life twice. Yet many who have been snatched from the jaws of death and danger return to a life of sin, as though they had never encountered God. You can enjoy the fruits of the power of God without encountering God. The case of the nine lepers repeats itself again and again.

One healing that helped me understand that physical healing is not the be all and end all of God's purpose was my young friend Harold. Thirty-one years old and his wife eight months pregnant, Harold contracted tetanus and was brought to hospital at the point of death. The doctors said to me, "Mrs. Bleasdell, we have done all we can. The rest is up to God. Pray for all you are worth. And even if he lives it will be at least five months before he could begin to function normally."

"We can pray, doctor," I replied. "And we begin right now."

That evening we celebrated a Mass in which the whole prayer community sought God's mercy on Harold's behalf. At the end of the Mass there was an explosion of joy and I interpreted it to mean that God had answered our prayer. And so it was. In five weeks, Harold was back at work, completely restored, with no signs of the infection that had threatened his life.

Some time thereafter, Harold and his wife were going through difficult times and he was very angry.

"Harold," I encouraged, "remember all that God has done for you."

"Auntie Babsie, I often wonder why you didn't just let me die. I would have been better off."

"Shhh, Harold," I said in horror. Then I turned to God, "O God, do not hold this sin against him."

From that moment, mere physical healing has not been enough for me. There is a quest in the depth of my soul to see men changed, transformed by the renewal of their minds and spirits into Christ Jesus.

Making Clouds Dance

During one of my visits to Jamaica, a priest took me to a school where there were 650 young people restless as young horses. He said, "You will speak to them." So they gathered outdoors in blazing hot sun. I looked at them and thought, "What can I do here?" But then I said to God, "I am under obedience. This man is your anointed. He's brought me here to speak to them, so I've got to do that. Lord, your son has put me in this position. You've got to honor me because I've got to honor him."

The children were shifting from one leg to the other and back again, baking in the sun. I looked up at the sky in prayer and saw some clouds way off in the distance. I thought, "God gave me authority over the work of his hands, and he says creation will delight in doing his will. Now, if I'm under obedience—I've got to obey this crazy priest—then God will have to honor me." So, still looking at the clouds, I whispered, "Come on, come on." To my great surprise, the clouds began to come along merrily. They moved like doves. Our God likes the spectacular. He doesn't act in secret. He took the cross of Calvary in the sight of the whole world. At the crossroads of the mountain, they hung him up, and above him, written in four languages, were the words, "This is Jesus, the King of the Jews." Wanting to engage the children in this, I prayed, "God, you're not going to let me down. You can't let me down."

Then I called on the children: "Hello, there!" They all looked. "I was brought here to bring the word of God to you. How many of you believe God is with us?" They looked uncertain, so I shouted, "Come on, is God with us?"

"Yes."

"Fine. The sun's hot, isn't it?"

"Y-e-e-e-e-s!"

"Now, some of you have an unfair advantage. Umbrellas cover only some of you and some of you remain uncovered. God doesn't like that. He wants to give the same to all his children. So please, close your umbrellas."

Every umbrella went down.

Under my breath I said, "C'mon God, now it's your turn!" Then to the children: "You see that cloud? God gave the Israelites a cloud in the desert. If that cloud can cover us, we'll have a great time together."

"Yeah!" they cheered.

I prayed quietly, "Okay, God, you said where two or more agree; and here we've got 650 of them agreeing with me. So come on, let's do it." And then aloud, to the clouds: "Come on, in the name of Jesus." Because I was talking aloud, the children were with me, and the clouds quickly danced our way, joined together, and covered the whole courtyard. Shade was over us, and the children began shouting, cheering. Six hundred and fifty voices rejoicing in the work of the Lord! I thought, "Glory to God, he's done it again. I'd better get on with whatever it is he wants me to do. Who knows how long this will last."

By that time I had noticed that many of the children were suffering from an ailment called pinkeye. Believing that God would heal their eyes, I asked them again, "Do you believe God is here?"

"Yes!" They were ready to believe anything.

"Now, those of you with pinkeye, God's going to heal it right away." So I prayed for healing, and before my eyes they were healed. Then I thought, "Now it's time to run. Amen. Let's go."

Our God is an amazing God. He says to us, "Say it and it will happen." But first we must become the presence of Jesus and appropriate the mind of God: "Be transformed by the renewal of your mind, that you may prove what is the will of God, what is good and acceptable and perfect" (Rm 12:2 RSVCE). God wants this.

I am the body of Christ. Why? Because Christ lives in me. My hands his hands. My eyes his eyes. My feet his feet. My heart is his heart. Christ dwells in me. Christ dwells in you. We can't let him down. We have to allow him to use our whole body as if it were his. The incredible truth is that God wants me and you to use his power, his might, everything that is his as if it were ours. He asks for our puny weakness that he might impart to us his glorious strength and majesty.

Don't Give the Devil Your Back

God wants a glorious exchange of might and power. I tried to teach this to my prayer group. One day a group of us went on a picnic. When I realized we needed to hurry back in time for the seven o'clock prayer meeting, I said, "We must go." I led the way back down the path through the bushes. At one point there was a grapefruit branch over the path, and as I stooped under it I heard, "Sssssssss."

I froze. "Oh, God," I thought, and beheld a king-size snake winding its way across the branch. Without moving I whispered to my companions, "Stop. A snake." Well, they took off like lightning, arms flailing, knees high. After running about a hundred feet, they looked back for me.

"Babs!" they called out. "Run!"

And I said, "I don't have to run, the snake's running."

The word of God says, "Stand still. Stand still and the devil will flee." The snake took off and my friends took off and I was the only one who stood still. Bob Mumford once defined a leader as one who walks in front to test for quicksand. If the leader goes down, the rest of the company knows not to follow. A leader lives in continual risk for the sake of the others. If you want to be a leader yet don't want to take any risks, step down. Let somebody else take over.

When my friends returned from their jog, we left for the church and I told them, "Tonight, this will be my talk: When we are in the prayer meeting where there are no snakes and no enemies, we sing, 'In the name of Jesus, in the name of Jesus we have the victory.' But when we are there with the snakes, we run! And the Word of God specifically says, 'Don't give the devil your back.' In Ephesians 6, the one place that's not covered—your head's covered, your feet are covered, your breast is covered—the one place that's not covered is your back. Never give the devil your back. Stand firm and see what the Lord your God will do. With the word of God in your throat he is mighty and glorious, and with the word of God in your hand, annihilate the foe."

Busting the Brothels

In our quiet, beautiful little town of Arima, five brothel houses rose up. Naturally there was an outcry. By doing some detective work, we discovered that some influential people had shares in these houses. The girls were being imported from Colombia. How does one fight worldly power?

The Word of God is a two-edged sword. So we decided to walk back and forth before the brothels with the Word of God in our hands and the praise of God in our throats. We prayed the mountain-moving rosary. We never passed those places again without stopping and proclaiming to the spirits of lust, "In the name of Jesus, be lifted up and thrown into the sea. It is written in Acts (cf. 1:20) 'let his encampment be desolate. May no one dwell in it.'" Every time I went for groceries I had to pass one of the brothels, so I would stop my car and say, "In the name of Jesus, let the gods of lust, who did not make heaven and earth, perish from this place and from beneath these heavens. For it is written, 'Every knee shall bow, in heaven, on earth, and under the earth, and every tongue confess, to the glory of God the Father: Jesus Christ is Lord!'" (cf. Phl 2:10–11).

One morning I was at home minding my own business when a member of the prayer group stopped by and asked me, "Do you know what's happening?"

"No," I answered.

"Look outside."

I looked and saw a large crowd gathered by the courthouse. "What happened?"

"The police raided all of the Colombian brothels, and the judge has passed an extradition order. They're all to be shipped out."

I said, "Glory to God, it is written—"

And everyone in the house chimed in, "every knee shall bow in heaven, on the earth, and under the earth, and every tongue confess, to the glory of God the Father: Jesus Christ is Lord!"

Another such interesting story is that when Father

Michael and his colleague Fr. Ian Taylor were in the seminary, they would go to the city every Sunday night and "execute the Word" outside a house of ill repute. Fire burned this house down to nothing. What happened there was like what happened at Jericho: God's sentence has been executed, and no one has been able to rebuild on the land since.

Ousting Tainted Government

When I read from cover to cover the pen-portrait of Jesus Christ, I am amazed at the helps that God has put in the Scriptures for us. We changed a whole government through prayer. We tried to change them for thirty years just by voting, and nothing happened. Finally we realized that we didn't have the power to do it; but God did. We started to walk the streets and proclaim the lordship of Jesus. The night before the election, we stood outside of every polling station proclaiming, "In the name of Jesus, justice will be done."

When the election results began coming in, I heard that the first district went to the opposition and my heart began to rejoice. I didn't care who the opposition was, I just wanted God to do something. I thought, whatever God does is right. The people will get the government they deserve. With God on our side, who can be against us?" When the third district in a row went down, I prayed, "This is not the work of human beings, this is your work. In your presence, all I can do is kneel down and worship."

Then I heard shouting and rejoicing in the streets. I kept praying. Out of thirty-six seats, the opposition won thirty-three. I didn't think it could happen like that—thirty-three seats in one fell swoop. I hadn't asked God for that, but he always gives more than we can ask or imagine.

God did it. Men had grown discouraged, but God toppled a thirty-year regime in one day.

We have other wars on our hands. In the name of Jesus, speak to the gods of lust, fornication, pornography, drugs, prostitution, incest, abortion, and murder, and tell them to get out. Tell them to bow down and worship Jesus Christ. Say it till the devil trembles. Walk through your son's room and claim it for Jesus Christ. Walk through your daughter's room and proclaim it a sanctuary from all the evils that assail her.

Dealing with Drug Addicts

We cannot just preach God's word, bring men to Christ, and leave them there. We've got to be shepherds to them; we've got to tend them. We look after drug addicts—who often bite the hand that feeds them. They keep us on our toes. Sometimes we become weary.

A few years ago, Father Michael Moses stopped at home and ran upstairs to get something. When he came back out a few minutes later, he discovered that he had left the back window down in his car, and a video camera that he had borrowed to do some work for the Church had been stolen. We knew that one of the drug addicts had stolen it, but, still, we were without a camera and needed to replace it.

Darkness and light work together in a strange way. One of the men came to us and said, "Father Mike, you lost a camera. I know where it is." He then told him who stole it, to whom the thief had sold it, and where it was. "You go there," he added. "I am risking my life telling you this. But every day you bless me. Every day you feed me. I just want to help you today. I am not stealing yet. Some day I might begin to steal. . . . Father Mike, thank you for what you do. Today I am going to do something for you that I have never done, but you do it for me every day." Father Mike looked at him, puzzled, and the man continued, "Every day you say to me, 'God bless you.' Today I say to you, go, Father, and may God bless you."

We went. We were amazed to find that the den of the drug addicts was only 150 yards from the town's main church. When we arrived, we told the men what we wanted, and they said no. So each day for five days we stopped back and repeated our request. Finally they said, "Father, if you give us $800, we'll give it back to you."

I was so angry. I said, "Excuse me? Not one cent. I am sorry. It's ours; you know it's ours; and I want it back. Besides, we've come to you every day, once a day, like vitamin pills. We've come in peace. We are begging you to give the camera back. Well, let me tell you, at this moment, this is the end of it. I am not coming back. We are not coming back. The next visitation you have will be from God! The God of heaven and earth will visit you!"

I turned away, and I thought, "Oh, my, how will I

summon God to visit these people?" Then I headed for Mass and prayed, "God, you said that if we walk in your footsteps, follow your way, pray, and remain faithful, they will be beggars, not us. Lord, we begged them for five days. The Gospel is out of order. Lord, you said that we are going to be givers and not beggars. Lord, right now we are beggars: the Gospel is out of order. You promised and I am expecting you to fulfill your promise."

That evening Father Mike put on his priestly garments, put the Blessed Sacrament in a monstrance, and led the entire prayer group through that village. We stopped outside every home. Father held up the monstrance and blessed the homes. One person asked us to come in, and Father went inside to bless that home. The little children ran into the streets as we sang, "He sent to say, he will be coming. Prepare your hearts . . ." Then we continued our procession, playing loudly an audio tape of the Pope leading the rosary.

The next morning a man came to our house and said to Father Michael, "Here is your camera."

Father wept. He invited the man into the house, telling him: "Boy, you are a baptized Catholic. You cannot live in this way. I'm going to pray with you for repentance. I'm going to pray with you for the power of God, the power of your baptism to break forth." So Father Mike prayed with the man and sent him on his way. We haven't heard the end of the story yet, but are expecting to see a great revolution if we continue to pray in the power of the Holy Spirit. We know we must learn to say with Jesus, "Forgive them, Father, for they know not what they do."

33

Places of Refuge

Frequently young women come to me pregnant and abandoned by their boyfriends. Their parents are angry and disappointed. Through counsel it often becomes clear that they are rebellious. In every case I try to rally the support of the family. In some cases the parents are willing to help and forgive in spite of their deep disappointment. In other cases, however, there is no one who can offer either the material or emotional support necessary.

I began to invite such impoverished girls to live with us and share our life, always with the secret hope that their own lives would be enriched by the experience. It didn't take long to realize that we did not have enough time to give them the individual attention they so desperately needed. I began to dream of a house especially for pregnant teenagers and battered women, and a staff committed to seeing them through their time of need.

I began talking this over with two young women who

had been spiritually reborn and nurtured in our community and who are now powerful prayer group leaders, Deborah DeRosia and Janet Daniel. We prayed together about this need for a long time.

One morning I was startled out of my sleep at five o'clock by the telephone ringing.

"Auntie Babsie, I have a house for you," a male voice said.

"Who are you?"

"My name is Kurban Ali." I had never met the man. I recognized that the name was Islamic.

"I cannot buy a house and I don't want your house. Good-bye, Mr. Ali."

This episode recurred every morning at five o'clock. After about a week of this I snapped at him, "Mr. Ali, I don't have money to buy a house. I do not want your house. Stop bugging me." I was going to slam the phone down, when he spoke.

"Auntie Babsie, won't you even come to see the house? It is perfectly suited to a prayer meeting."

My temper yielded to curiosity. The words "prayer meeting" were exactly the words to soften my heart.

Mr. Ali told me that my name had come to him while he was praying—which he did every morning at five. Perhaps the God of Abraham, who was also my God, was at work again. He gave me the address and confided that he was asking $225,000 for this house, but this was negotiable.

I called Deborah and Janet and we went to see the house. At the end of a quiet cul-de-sac, the house was ideal for the privacy necessary to shelter women. It could also be ideal as a central point of evangelization for that area. We negotiated a reduced price of $175,000 with a down payment of $50,000 and possession in two months. We bonded ourselves together immediately to bring together all of our available financial resources for this effort.

But in the lawyer's office Mr. Ali declared that the $50,000 was only to seal the bargain. He would not relinquish the house until we had paid every cent. We told Mr. Ali to forget the whole deal. After some prayer we decided to look for another house.

The next morning the ritual of the early telephone calls resumed. Mr. Ali was determined to drive me nuts! His elephant hide was impervious to my outrage and disgust.

In the meantime, I had written to a friend of mine in England, casually telling her about the community's activities. In my letter I had written that we needed $100,000 to buy a halfway house for women in need.

In the midst of our search for another house, I received a telephone call from this woman. "Babsie," she greeted me, "about that $100,000 . . . do you still need it?"

"What? I wasn't asking you for $100,000."

"No, I know. But do you still need it? Do you want it?"

I hemmed and hawed.

"Babsie, hurry up, this is long distance. I just happen to have ended up with more money in Trinidad than I ever dreamed of. Suppose I were to give you an interest-free loan; would you accept it? You can decide the terms of repayment."

"Would I accept it?" I gasped. "With deepest gratitude; and we will set ourselves to the task of finding the money for repayment."

"Okay. I will instruct my financiers to get in touch with you and you can work it out with them. I wish I could just give it to you. But my children would not understand that at this point. I hope they will one day come to the place where they will agree." She, like me, had only two daughters, and she was a widow.

Within a few days her lawyers and accountants summoned me to their offices. They were incredulous when I suggested that this would have to be a "faith loan" since we had no financial credit, no regular cash flow, no predictable income. I was living entirely by faith, and God had been faithful. The lawyers and financiers could not comprehend this at all. The more I tried to explain to these hard-knuckled financial magnates, the more ridiculous it seemed, even to me. Finally they told me to go home and they would think about it. Even though the money wasn't theirs, they said, they had a responsibility to protect it. I left laughing.

A few days later they called me back and asked me if I would accept a personal loan, even though, as an uninsured sixty-five-year-old woman, I was completely unqualified.

"Are you willing to do it?" I asked. "If you are willing, I am ready."

I left with a check in my hand made out to Ursula Bleasdell for $100,000. And I signed a note promising to repay it in five yearly installments of $20,000 each. I was confident that the three prayer communities could hold an annual bazaar and raise the money to honor this.

Soon Mr. Ali's house was ours. With the help of the community we set up housekeeping. In prayer we arrived at the name "Goshen," since the house was to be a place of rest and restoration just as the land of Goshen in Egypt was the place where Jacob and his sons found refuge.

Immediately after we opened the house, rumors of recession hit the country. Our dollar was devalued by thirty per cent. Terror crept into my heart. How would we ever be able to raise $20,000 dollars from poor people hit by recession? How could I ever have been foolish enough to believe that I could pull off this financial feat? Would I have to betray my friend? Would I embarrass her before her children? Would she regret coming to our assistance?

The confusion was compounded when I received a letter from her. Six months had transpired since the loan; I was sure she was writing to remind me of my commitment to repay. My courage failed me. I could not open the letter, so I stuck it on a shelf in my bedroom. Every time I entered the room, the blue airmail envelope assaulted my vision and I would cry out to God, "Save me, Lord. Do not let me be put to shame."

Everyone who came into the room would ask, "Why aren't you opening that letter?"

"That letter? I'm waiting for the energy to deal with the contents."

One day about a month later, as I entered the room, a

surge of energy flooded me and I reached out and picked up the letter. Whatever it said, I was ready. I slit it open and read the first line:

"Dear Babsie, I suppose that by now you have heard from my financiers . . ."

"Oh, Lord," I gasped. "Just as I feared!"

The letter continued. "I have *absolved* you the loan. Babsie, do you understand? You owe me nothing."

It was more than I could take. I slumped to a sitting position on my bed. A community member entered the room and observed my stupor.

"Auntie Babsie, are you all right? What is the matter?"

Without a word I handed her the letter. As she read, she flashed like a neon sign. Her pale complexion began flashing red and then white and then red again.

"Do you understand?" I asked. "Do you understand what the matter is?"

"Oo oohh, oo oohh! Praise God! Praise God!"

We laughed and danced as on the day of Pentecost. I felt as if a noose had been cut from around my neck. The prison of fear gave way to the explosive freedom of faith and trust in the ability of God to do anything. And of course our gratitude extended to my beloved friend in faraway England, who was my gift from him!

If freedom from financial debt can bring such joy, how is it that freedom from the debt of sin through Jesus Christ does not yield higher dividends? I still wonder. Perhaps I shall never find an answer to this question until he returns again in glory.

House of Grace

It didn't take long for our work in Goshen to get going. But something overtook us that we hadn't anticipated. The adult population was transient, but we found ourselves responsible for a resident population of thirteen abandoned children from unexpected sources. Children would come seeking refuge for a day or a week and remain with us forever, or so it seemed. A whole new ministry blossomed. We had to provide for the children food, shelter, clothing, education, health care, and emotional and spiritual support.

We now have a second house entirely for children, which we have named "The House of Grace," under the patronage of our Lady of Grace. I recalled my dream of many years ago in which a large procession was walking straight past the statue of our Lady and I promised her that I would never pass her straight, but would always say "Hello."

Another financial miracle from friends in America made it possible for us to acquire this house in an outright cash purchase. The owner reduced the price of the house out of deference to the work we were doing and in thanksgiving for the healing of her six-year-old son from a bone disease some eighteen years prior. When I telephoned to inquire about the house for sale, the boy who had been healed answered the phone himself.

Currently one of our most precious occupants of the House of Grace is Lawrence, a little boy we found in a hovel abandoned to the care of a senile grandmother.

Every crevice of the house was sealed with newsprint, shutting out all air and light. For all intents and purposes this eight-year-old child was deaf, dumb, and blind. When he was held up by Sister Paule Clarke, the Dominican sister who discovered him, his legs and arms just dangled. He could not even stand or sit on his own. Only his head and teeth had grown normally. When we took him to the doctor, he said, "It's obvious that this child is very hungry. There is nothing that I can even suggest now except food and tender loving care. You never know what that can accomplish. We will see him again later on."

Lawrence is now fourteen and a real little person. The first faculty to develop was his hearing, and then his sight. As his limbs grew strong, he began to walk two years later at the age of ten. He still doesn't speak, but he whistles, and it's a joy to hear him whistle. He can hold a cup, but he still takes only liquid. Father Michael conditionally baptized him, presuming that he had never been baptized. Later Father decided that Lawrence could receive his first holy Communion.

All the other children in the household go to school, and one of them has just begun secondary school. One boy has completed technical school with the Benedictine monks and is now a fine cabinet maker, living on his own. Another boy is doing a course in barbering and another is now a plumber. One of our girls is a qualified dressmaker. Two children are in kindergarten and the others are in primary school.

There are so many thousands of homeless children that I often ponder how the Lord will raise up enough houses to care for them. But I remember that salvation is the work of Jesus in us and not of ourselves. I humbly pray with the whole Church, "Father, yours is the vineyard, yours is the harvest. You assign the task and pay a wage that is just. Help me to be faithful to all of my responsibilities today and never let me be separated from your love."

34

Baby's Change of Address

I was in Arkansas with John Michael Talbott's community, Little Portion, to do a weekend conference. When I left home my sister, Baby, who had been ailing over a period of months, was due for an extensive internal examination. So before going to the conference site I telephoned to find out if they had any results. My brother-in-law reported that she was diagnosed with terminal cancer of the liver. She was only expected to live for two months.

I felt as if a sword pierced my heart. I said to God, "I have to stand up and say how good you are. I have to stand up and boast about your power. I cannot stand before the people and weep. That would give you no glory. So, therefore, send your anointing." I went back to the bus and we started off.

The thing I wanted most was a place to be quiet, to internalize what it really meant to have my only sister under such a diagnosis. I consoled myself by thinking that as soon as I got to the hotel I would go to my room and in privacy I would pray. But when we got to the hotel the desk informed me that they couldn't find the key to my room, so I would have to wait a little while. At that moment my eyes strayed to a low concrete wall. I thought I could sit there quietly behind one of the pillars and receive an anointing from God, peace, and the power to speak of his goodness.

As soon as I sat down I saw a woman coming toward me. "Not one second to myself," I thought. "Not one second for me to get in touch with myself. Oh, God, all I want is a place of quiet. Will you deny me that?" But the lady was standing right in front of me by this time. I looked at her and smiled because I knew God would want me to. Then I stretched out my hand and said, "Do you want to talk to me?"

"You're Babsie Bleasdell. I saw your name in the letter. I came here in the hope that I could talk to you."

I took both her hands in mine and said, "Tell me."

"I have waited two years to talk to you. You were in New Orleans two years ago, weren't you? You remember the healing service on the Saturday night?"

"I don't think I will ever forget it."

"That night," she said, "I went to New Orleans in terminal cancer. And when they called for people with cancer to come up for prayers I went straight to you and you prayed with me. I was slain in the Spirit for a long time; I don't know how long. But when I got up I was completely healed. Today, two years after, I am healthier than I have ever been in my whole life. I wanted to let you know and to thank you."

A wave of hope surged through me. I squeezed her hands and said, "Thank you. I didn't need that news two years ago. I didn't need it two hours ago. I needed it now. I just received the news that my own sister is in terminal cancer."

She looked at me and said, "I'm sorry."

"No, no," I assured her. "Thank you for bringing that word of consolation. What I have heard you say is that God says, 'Pray. Prayer still works. But if I do not act the way you expect me to, know this, I am still doing for you the most loving thing that I can do at this moment.'"

As soon as I could, I returned home to my sister to look after her. One night I was so tired I felt as if I couldn't take another step. I had been looking after Baby at night and working by day. "Lord," I said, "I am going to scream. I'm at the end of my tether. If I scream, my sister will be reproached and the whole family will say that I only know how to praise you when I am not in trouble, so you will get no mileage out of that. You promised me peace. I'm going to sit down here and not get up until you flood my soul with peace." So I sat down and continued, "Lord, I'm serious. You promised me peace that surpasses all understanding." Then the Lord poured his peace on me. I got up and ministered to Baby every day and every night until she died. Never again did I feel discouraged. The anointing of God saw me through.

There was amazing grace right through to the bitter end—which endures up to this time and enables me to think of my sister, not as dead, but as having changed her address for a better place. When I sent out the intimation of her death I wrote on it, "Change of Address. My sister Callistra passed from her local address to the eternal arms of Jesus on August 28, 1993." Then I put "Former Location: Earth" and "New Location: The Arms of Jesus Forever." Everyone said that it was very effective in bringing alive to them the reality that death is merely the beginning of new life.

Since Baby's death, my well-meaning charismatic friends have been telling me, "You have to cry. You see, you must grieve."

"But," I say, "God has ministered to me."

"No, no, no, no, no. Grief has twelve steps. You must go through the twelve steps of grieving."

And I tell them again, "But God has ministered to me."

They ring me up: "You are much too quiet. You must grieve. She's your only sister."

Finally, I say, "Okay, fine. Let's settle this. I am going to tell God, 'Lord, why have you brought me to step twelve? I should only be at step four.'"

That puts an end to their arguments. They leave me alone now. I hope that they have come to realize that God is not tied to a schedule. He is bigger than schedules. God is not tied to a program. In his infinite mercy he gives us schedules and programs to help us out in our finite state. But God himself is not tied to these things. He wants to do exceedingly, abundantly more than we can ask for or imagine, if only we would turn to him and say, "Lord, I believe, help thou my unbelief." The mercy of God is infinite because God does not want a dead people on his hands. He wants a people full, exuberant with the life of the Holy Spirit. As St. Irenaeus wrote: "The glory of God is man fully alive."

35

In the Fullness of Time

I never thought God would use my life the way he has used it. God is never short on surprises. God loves each one of us individually, as if there were no one else to love. He wants us to take on family characteristics, family traits so that we will be easily recognized.

Ephesians tells us that we are called to grow in grace and glory until we reflect God himself. In other words, each of us is intended by God to be a shadow of God. When you see an airplane shadow, you can usually tell that an airplane is flying overhead without looking up. If you were to see a kite shadow, you wouldn't mistake it for an airplane. So God hopes that through us he will become visible as we take on his traits and characteristics.

God hopes that each of us will become a citizen of the kingdom of God. Hell wasn't prepared for us but for the devil and his angels. God has prepared another place for us. Jesus told us: "I go to prepare a place for you, and when it is ready I will come back for you" (cf. Jn 14:3).

Every day of my life, every moment of my life, is spent acting out what God has done—my response to the love of God. I experience myself as a debtor. I understand what God has saved me from. There were moments in my life during which, if God had called me from this life, I would have gone to hell. But he waited for me. And he watched over me. And he saved me. Many times Jesus must have wept over me as he wept over Jerusalem. But he never gave up because he could look at me and know his plan and purpose for me. He had faith in his own power to bring me someday to a place where I could look at him and say, "What do you want of me?"

When we serve God, we never know what name we will get. Father Duffy once told me, "In North America I am known as the priest who prayed over Babsie Bleasdell." It's amazing. This mighty man of God came all the way to the sleepy little town of Arima, Trinidad, to my own living room, prayed over me, and twenty-five years later he is known not as the priest who prophesies and does marvelous things, but as the priest who prayed over Babsie Bleasdell. We never know what God wants to do, but we do know that if we are faithful to his call, all generations shall call us blessed.

Mary's answer to God was, "Be it done unto me according to thy word." That is the key. God's power comes to us when we say yes. Mary's "yes" has reverberated through two thousand years, and every day in the prayer of the Church it is repeated as an example for us. I believe in my heart that each one of us is being called in these prophetic times. The Scriptures say: "In the fullness of time God brought forth his Son" (cf. Gal 4:4). In the fullness of time God called forth Babsie Bleasdell. In the fullness of time God calls you.